Keeping the University Free and Growing

Keeping the University Free and Growing

By Herman Lee Donovan
President, University of Kentucky
1941–1956

UNIVERSITY OF KENTUCKY PRESS

COPYRIGHT © 1959 BY THE UNIVERSITY OF KENTUCKY PRESS

THE LIBRARY OF CONGRESS HAS CATALOGED THIS BOOK AS:

Donovan, Herman Lee, 1887–
 Keeping the university free and growing. [Lexington]
University of Kentucky Press [1959]
 162 p. illus. 23 cm.

1. Kentucky. University.   I. Title.

LD2762.D6   378.769   59–6960 ‡

Library of Congress

To
NELL STUART DONOVAN
who served without salary on
the staff of the presidency as
hostess of Maxwell Place

FOREWORD

HERMAN LEE DONOVAN was President of the University of Kentucky from July 1, 1941, to August 31, 1956. The intervening years witnessed tremendous advances in both the scope and the quality of the University's program. In a sense it can be said that the institution came to maturity during this period.

However, it was not an easy fifteen years. The educational problems growing out of World War II and the avalanche of veteran students that followed were many and difficult. And they were by no means the only problems. Throughout the entire period the costs of nearly everything the University needed were on the rise. By and large, the people of Kentucky were still unaware of the meaning of a "great university," and therefore heedless of its needs. Some in positions of leadership in the State were only partially sympathetic with the concept of the "free university." In summary, the administration of the University was characterized by one crisis after another, many of them major. This is not to say that it was an unhappy period for Dr. Donovan or for his University associates. There were, in fact, many pleasant and joyous occasions, and many opportunities for rejoicing. But it was a battle all the way.

And therein, perhaps, lies the explanation of President Donovan's success. He loved the University of Kentucky, as deeply perhaps as any man ever associated with it, and he was most happy when he could do battle on its behalf. Though a thoughtful student of education, he was essentially a man of action. He took little stock in the belief that problems often will solve themselves if let alone. He preferred rather to face the issues as they arose. After careful analysis of a situation, and after consultation with his colleagues, he decided on a course of action and took the offensive. He was inclined neither to procrastinate nor to allow the University to be put on the defensive. He had ample courage; and though realistic and reasonably resilient, he rarely, if ever, compromised on a matter of principle.

Soon he won the confidence and loyalty of a vast majority of the faculty. Gradually he made the people of the State aware of their University and its possibilities. Gradually he convinced every adversary that the University was going forward and that it was to remain a free institution in every regard and in the fullest meaning of that term.

The material evidences of the University's progress are many, but the greatest contributions of the Donovan administration were perhaps those less tangible—a genuine university atmosphere, the improved status of the faculty, the enlarged and strengthened graduate program, the accelerated pace of research, the general elevation of standards, and the progress made against unwarranted interference in the management of the institution and against any infringement of freedom of learning and teaching.

In *Keeping the University Free and Growing*, Dr. Donovan has not sought to write a history of his administration or to evaluate it. This task, he knows, must await the future historian with the necessary perspective. Dr. Donovan has, however, made the task of that historian immeasurably easier, by recording for him those intimate experiences and personal reactions that will give life and spirit to what otherwise might be a mere recital of events.

Out of his rich experience the author too has revealed, as few have done before, the day-to-day life of a university president with its tribulations, its penalties, and its rewards. Finally, he has set forth a philosophy of administration that should be of material benefit to present and future generations of college presidents.

Leo M. Chamberlain
Vice President of the
University of Kentucky

PREFACE

FOR TWENTY-EIGHT YEARS as a college president I prepared a written report for each meeting of the trustees. Always I discussed some aspect of the educational program of the institution, some problems under consideration or plans achieved. The purpose of these reports was to create a better understanding of the work of the institution; and they were put into writing in order to make each of them a matter of record.

When I retired as President of the University of Kentucky, I conceived the idea of preparing a report directed to the members of the Board of Trustees, the professors, and the general public. This report was designed to summarize the principal activities, achievements, and problems of the University during the years of my administration from 1941 to 1956. Not all the achievements of the University during this period, nor all the problems, are discussed. The problems considered are those that offered the greatest challenge to the President and his colleagues. While other problems consumed much of our time, it is the more crucial ones that have been reviewed in this survey.

The reader must not regard this book as an autobiography, though it necessarily contains some autobiographical material. Nor is it a history of the period, though it contains considerable historical material useful to a future historian of the University. The book is primarily a report on the major problems that one college president encountered, how squarely he faced them, and how he tried to solve them.

The first acknowledgment I would make is to Hal Price Headley and members of the Board of Directors of the Keeneland Foundation for the grant of $4,000 for the publication of this report. In the years I served as President I never made a

PREFACE

financial request of this foundation but that it was granted; and the total of these gifts ran into thousands of dollars.

To the faculty and staff of the University I shall be forever indebted for their cooperation and faithful support. The credit is largely due to them for whatever success the University has had over these years.

Specifically, I wish to acknowledge my indebtedness to Vice President Leo Chamberlain for carefully reading the manuscript, and to Vice President Frank D. Peterson and his staff for assistance in gathering materials. Also, I am under obligation to the late Professor Ezra L Gillis for the statistical data which he so carefully assembled during the period of my presidency. To my former secretary, Miss Lucy Hogan, I am deeply indebted for checking this manuscript as to errors. To no one am I under greater obligation than to Dr. Jacob D. Farris of the University Health Service, my personal physician, who has guarded my health so that I might have strength to carry on the strenuous life of a college president.

I desire also to express my indebtedness to the fifty-two trustees who served terms on the fifteen-man Board of Trustees during the years of my administration, 1941-1956. I am proud to say that these trustees never rejected a recommendation which I made to them. They deserve great credit for their unselfish and consecrated service to the University of Kentucky. It is altogether fitting that this preface should present the names of these trustees:

EX-OFFICIO MEMBERS

Governors: Keen Johnson, Simeon S. Willis, Earle C. Clements, Lawrence W. Wetherby, Albert B. Chandler.

Superintendents of Public Instruction: John Brooker,† John Fred Williams, Boswell B. Hodgkin, Wendell P. Butler, Robert Martin.

Commissioners of Agriculture: W. H. May, Harry F. Walters,† Elliott Robertson, Ben S. Adams, Ben Butler.

APPOINTED MEMBERS

Richard C. Stoll,*† James Park, John Sherman Cooper, Horace S. Cleveland, Louis E. Hillenmeyer, Marshall Barnes, Lee Kirk-

† Deceased   * Chairman of Executive Committee

patrick,† Robert Tway, H. D. Palmore, Grover Creech,† Thomas H. Cutler, John C. Everett,† Eldred E. Adams, J. N. Smith, Edward C. O'Rear, Guy A. Huguelet,*† W. M. Coffee, George M. Cheek, J. Woodward Howard, Herndon J. Evans, Paul M. Basham, Thomas W. Ballantine, Smith D. Broadbent, Marion W. Moore, Harper Gatton, R. P. Hobson,* Mrs. Paul G. Blazer, Carl Dempewolfe,† Ralph J. Angelucci, J. Stephen Watkins, Robert C. Stilz, Harry Denham, Louis Cox, Daniel E. Elkin, William F. Foster, Wood Hannah.

The administrative deans of the several colleges constituted the cabinet of the President, and I depended on them for advice and help in the administration of the University. These were stalwart men, scholarly and dynamic.

This roll includes the following persons to whom I am indebted for whatever success the University has had during the period 1941-1956.

College of Arts and Sciences: Dean Paul P. Boyd, Dean M. M. White.

College of Agriculture and Home Economics: Dean Thomas Poe Cooper,† Dean Frank J. Welch.

College of Engineering: Dean James H. Graham, Dean Daniel V. Terrell.

College of Law: Dean Alvin E. Evans,† Dean Elvis J. Stahr.

College of Education: Dean William S. Taylor,† Dean Frank G. Dickey.

College of Commerce: Dean Edward Wiest, Dean C. C. Carpenter.

College of Pharmacy: Dean Earl P. Slone.

Graduate School: Dean W. D. Funkhouser,† Dean Louis Pardue, Dean Herman E. Spivey.

Lexington, Kentucky
October 1, 1958

H. L. D.

CONTENTS

	PAGE
Foreword, by Leo M. Chamberlain	vii
Preface	ix

CHAPTER
1. The Role of the University President 1
2. Financing the University Program 15
3. Emergency Building for a University 28
4. Relations with Faculty and Staff 37
5. New Colleges and Departments 46
6. When a University Goes to War 56
7. Public Relations of the University 60
8. Keeping the University Free 69
9. The Vanishing University Trustee 79
10. Student Citizenship on the Campus 85
11. Integration at the University 95
12. The Athletics Program of the University 102
13. The University's Library Facilities 117
14. The University Press and Foundations 122
15. A University President Views Three Professions 126

APPENDIX
 A. Tables 1-4 137
 B. Athletic Association Documents 140
 C. Reading Assignment for College Presidents 145

Index 157

CHAPTER ONE

The Role of the University President

ON April 1, 1941, the Board of Trustees of the University of Kentucky met in Lexington and appointed me President of the University. During the next fifteen years I never had a day without its problems, most of them minor, some major and exceedingly harassing. There were decisions to be made that gave me genuine pleasure, and others that cut me like a knife. But there was no way to escape the unpleasant choices without injuring the University. I had to say *no* to requests much more frequently than to say *yes*, for if I had acceded to every demand, the University's resources soon would have been dissipated and the institution left bankrupt.

On July 1, 1941, I assumed the duties of President, being cordially received by the general public and courteously accepted by the faculty. However, many members of the faculty were none too well pleased with my appointment by the trustees. In the first place, the trustees had not requested the faculty's help in selecting the new President, although a faculty-trustee committee had been appointed to make recommendations. Secondly, the University was still in the depression and salaries were very low, so that the faculty were uneasy over their economic status. Finally, at the time of my appointment the Board of Trustees abolished the University Senate, which included both professors and administrators, and established in its place a University Faculty, made up exclusively of administrative officers and deans, to be the governing body of the University. This action lowered the morale of many professors.

There was reason for this action by the trustees. During the last year of President Frank McVey's administration a number of dissatisfied professors had caucused before each meeting of the University Senate on problems and policies that were to be considered by that body, and had voted as a bloc on practically all questions coming before it. The trustees became convinced that the University Senate was no longer a deliberative body and should be abolished.

When notified of my appointment as President, I did not know that the Board had abolished the University Senate. Had I been informed of this action, I probably would not have accepted the position.

On the morning of July 1, 1941, I walked from Maxwell Place, the official residence of the President, to my office, where half a dozen friends greeted me. A few minutes later I was working at my desk on the agenda prepared for my consideration. Since the items of business were familiar to me, the office did not feel strange and I did not have to seek advice in order to answer the queries presented to me. I was taking up at the University the routine that I had left at Eastern Kentucky State Teachers' College, where I had been president for thirteen years. The chief difference, I soon discovered, between the presidency at Eastern and at the University was that at the University there were more problems of greater complexity to face. Also, greater pressures were placed upon the President of the University both from within and from without.

When I was appointed president of Eastern in 1928, I thought over how I could best prepare myself for the new work. After some consideration I decided to study the biographies and autobiographies of some successful college presidents, to learn how they had handled their problems. This decision resulted in my reading David Starr Jordan's autobiography, *Days of a Man;* William Allen Neilson's biography of Charles W. Eliot; the autobiography of Andrew D. White; and Thomas W. Goodspeed's biography of William Rainey Harper. From the experience of these older and wiser men who had directed the destinies of great universities, I received much help and inspiration. Before long I found myself a collector of the biographies of college and university presidents; and from the continued study of my treasured collection (see Appendix C) I gathered strength to meet the problems that challenged and sometimes almost baffled me.

My first task was to rectify the Board of Trustees' action in abolishing the University Senate, for I was sure that the University could not be operated successfully with any such legislative body as the Board had provided. This would be a delicate matter to handle, for both professors and trustees had strong feelings on the subject. Time was required to reconcile the thinking of both groups.

From the Board of Trustees I secured permission to appoint a committee, which we called the Committee of Fifteen, to prepare governing regulations for the University. This committee, composed of three deans and twelve professors, was to make a careful investigation of the subject and report to the President, and through him to the trustees. The chairman of the committee was Dean Thomas P. Cooper, of the College of Agriculture, who for the preceding year had been Acting President of the University. The committee studied the subject carefully for more than a year before reporting to the President.

When I presented the report to the trustees, I recommended that it be approved. To my surprise there was much unfavorable comment in the discussion. I saw that if the issue came to a vote, it would be turned down, and so I obtained permission to withdraw the report. From time to time I talked to individual members of the Board of Trustees about the necessity of studying this matter of governing regulations for the University, but they were reluctant to approve the recommendations of the Committee of Fifteen. Finally, at an executive meeting of the trustees on April 6, 1943, I made as earnest a plea as I knew how to make, giving reasons why it was important to reconsider the committee's recommendations and not run the risk of incurring the disfavor of accrediting agencies and the ridicule of other universities.

Then Judge Richard C. Stoll, who had been a trustee for nearly half a century, spoke up. "I do not believe in what you are recommending, but since you appear to be so deeply interested in it, I move that the report be approved." The motion was carried unanimously, and the governing regulations were soon put into effect.

This achievement seems to me one of the outstanding accomplishments of my years as President of the University. The governing regulations grew out of the wisdom of deans and professors after much patient study. They were produced through a democratic process in which administrators, professors, and trustees each made their contribution. There have been two revisions of the original study, and from time to time amendments have been made as the growing University's problems have become more complex. Under the guidance of Vice President Leo Chamberlain the regulations were reedited in 1955 and published in their present form.

The adoption of a sound code of governing regulations giving every employee of the University a clear-cut statement of his rights, privileges, responsibilities, and duties, as well as the relation of his position to others in the organization, has done much to improve the morale of the professors and others employed by the University. It has also resulted in giving the trustees a clearer concept of their function and responsibilities. When the question arises as to whether some issue should be resolved by the University Faculty or by the trustees, a reference to the governing regulations of the Board of Trustees will usually provide the answer.

What are the outstanding duties and responsibilities of the president of a state university? How does his work today differ from that of a university president fifty, seventy-five, or a hundred years ago? This question can be answered in part by comparing my work in the years 1941-1956 with that of a former President of this University.

James K. Patterson was President of the University of Kentucky from 1869 to 1910. Our records are very complete in regard to President Patterson's duties. They reveal the following facts as to his activities: The President prepared the budget of the institution with the approval of the trustees, and then presented it to the Governor and the General Assembly of the State, doing such lobbying as was necessary to secure its approval. This burden President Patterson carried without much assistance. This has continued to be a presidential activity to the present day, although we receive more assistance from others than did President Patterson. With his own hands he prepared the annual catalog and was responsible for the courses offered, for in the old days this was not a function of the faculty. He interviewed every student entering the University and personally made out each student's schedule of classes. With a clerk's assistance he recorded in his office all student grades at the end of a term. He was the personnel officer of the University, the adviser of every student on matters about which the student wanted advice—or on which the President thought the student needed advice. He handled every disciplinary problem that arose in the school, and meted out justice according to his own standards of discipline. He employed every worker connected with the institution and to a limited degree supervised his work, whether in academic or in service fields. He inspected for approval every bill submitted to the University, and countersigned all checks. He served as his own superintendent of buildings and grounds, planting the trees and shrubs where he thought they ought to be planted.

In addition to these duties, he presided over the daily chapel meeting, over convocations, and over all faculty meetings held on the campus. He usually taught classes in history or in classical languages. He answered personally all correspondence coming to his office. He was the University's public-relations officer. He prepared with the approval of the trustees all educational policies controlling the University. He made speeches in many parts of the State, often he attended public meetings as the representative of the University, and when he was not busied about all these things, he frequently prepared educational editorials and comments on international affairs upon invitation of the editor of the Louisville *Courier-Journal.* His administration of the University has been recognized as a benevolent dictatorship. He was a kindly man who in his later years walked with the aid of a crutch and a cane, but ever a fighter who apparently never tried to avoid a controversy.

President Patterson and his colleagues of half a century ago did personally many of the things which we as university presidents today delegate to others. Many of the functions of our office today are the same as those of an earlier time, but we have extended the office by the use of assistants who work for us. The state-university president has multiplied his services many times over through the creation of the offices of vice president, dean, registrar, comptroller, personnel director, director of public relations, director of athletics, director of libraries, director of placement service, and others. This change constitutes the most significant difference between the presidency of then and now.

It may be of interest to the public to learn how deans and professors in their manual define the duties of the President of the University of Kentucky today:

> The President of the University is the executive officer of the institution and of all the work associated with it, and ex officio a member of all faculties. As such executive officer, he shall have full charge of the administrative activities of the University; and the Vice President, the Vice President (Business Administration), the Provost, all deans and directors, and all other subordinate officers and employees of the University shall be subject to his supervision and direction. He shall also serve as the official medium of communication between the Board of Trustees, on the one hand, and the University Faculty, administrative officers, individual members of the faculty and staff, student organizations, and students, on the other. He is responsible to the Board for administering the educational and business policies of the institution, subject only to the law

THE ROLE OF THE UNIVERSITY PRESIDENT 7

and the University rules and regulations prescribed by the Board of Trustees.

The President shall call meetings of the University Faculty and of the Assembly and shall preside over them. He may also call meetings of the various college faculties. It is the duty of the President to make recommendations relating to the general policies of the institution and to the maintenance of coordination among its several functions.

It is the function of the President to see that the rules and regulations of the Board of Trustees and of the University Faculty are enforced. It is also his duty, directly or through the various University officers, to administer (a) all budgetary matters (other than approval of the budget by the Board of Trustees), including all business and financial activities; (b) all personnel matters, including appointments, promotions, transfers, changes of pay, retirement, and staff discipline; (c) the application of University rules relating to studies; (d) the admission and classification of students; (e) registrations and class assignments; (f) curricula and courses of study; (g) research and teaching; (h) all physical facilities, including buildings and grounds, libraries, laboratories, et cetera; (i) University commencements and other convocations; (j) student discipline; (k) student activities; (l) student social life; (m) University publications; (n) the University calendar and modifications in it; (o) public relations; (p) athletics and military training; and to perform all other administrative functions, whether expressly enumerated herein or not, necessary or appropriate for the effective operation of the University.

A comparison of the work of Dr. Patterson as President with the outline of duties of the President of the University today as enumerated by the Committee of Fifteen will reveal many activities in common. However, present-day presidents have to face new responsibilities. The greatest difference between the work President Patterson performed and the work I did as President of the University was primarily in degree and tempo. Things moved more slowly in President Patterson's day. There were fewer committee meetings and conferences; if a decision was to be made, he usually made it. There were fewer professors and not so many students, and their demands were fewer, their wants simpler. The pressures on the President were not so great. This is not to say that the President was not a busy man. He was indeed busy; but life, all in all, was less strenuous in the late nineteenth century than it is today.

The presidency during Patterson's four decades consisted of one man and a secretary. Today the presidency comprises a number of men and women under a leader called the president. He, the president, has multiplied himself many times over by the use of others to whom he delegates specific responsibilities. Presidents of an earlier day were essentially dictators, whose authority was seldom challenged or resented, since such was the accepted way of administering the office. Perhaps earlier presidents would not have known how to delegate authority, since that technique had not yet been developed to any degree in educational institutions. Because the university leader has learned the art of delegation, the office of president today is likely to be more efficiently carried on than ever before. The president now employs techniques learned from business; he is more of an executive, less of a professor or preacher.

During the fifteen years when I served as President, I recommended to the Board of Trustees the creation of three vice-presidencies and the directorships of the personnel office, public relations, University press, libraries, placement service, and athletics. The offices of dean of the various colleges and of men and of women had been established by my predecessors. These administrative positions constitute a part of the presidency. In a complex institution such as a state university, which enrolls several thousand persons and employs a faculty and staff of more than two thousand persons, it is imperative that the presidency comprise a number of highly competent persons prepared professionally to administer the colleges, schools, departments, divisions, and business organization. Each of these administrative persons represents a part of the presidency, and to each of these individuals the president delegates certain functions formerly discharged by the president himself.

At the time of my appointment as President of the University, the Board of Trustees established the position of dean of the University. They did this because they were convinced that the office of President was understaffed. They directed me to find a competent assistant to whom I could delegate a part of the administrative burden. It did not take me long to decide upon the man I wanted for this new position, Dr. Henry H. Hill, who at one time had been a professor in the College of Education in the University, and who then was associate superintendent of schools in St. Louis, Missouri. Because I regarded Dr. Hill as one of the best administrators I had ever known, I considered no other person for the deanship. I offered him the position two minutes after we met, and he accepted as promptly. Thus began a most delightful partnership in administration. It lasted only one year, however. The board of education of Pittsburgh, Pennsylvania, offered him twice the salary that the University of Kentucky was paying him. Dr. Hill did not like to leave our University; he said to me seriously, "Tell me you cannot accept my resignation because I have been on this job too short a time. I do not wish to leave here." My reply was, "You cannot afford to stay. You would be making too much of a sacrifice. Besides, you owe it to your family to accept the larger salary." Reluctantly Dr. Hill accepted the Pittsburgh position, which he left four years later to head George Peabody College for Teachers.

During my first year at the University, I discovered that Dr. Leo Chamberlain, at that time registrar, was one of the ablest and most scholarly men on the institution's staff. When Dr. Hill left, I at once asked Dr. Chamberlain to become dean of the University (now Vice President). Fourteen years, in season and out, we worked together, never at any time having a disagreement. We had somewhat the same philosophy of education; we agreed on the objectives of the University; and our ideas of what constituted good administration were similar. He was an incessant worker, calm in judgment, quiet in manner, and courageous when courage was needed. When I was off the campus, he acted as President. Twice when I was in Europe for a considerable period of time, he was wholly responsible for the administration of the institution.

At the time I was appointed President, the Board of Trustees appointed Frank D. Peterson as comptroller. Later I recommended that his title be changed to Vice President in charge of Business Affairs (now Vice President of Business Administration). Mr. Peterson had served for some years as the chief financial officer of the State Department of Education, Frankfort, Kentucky. He had also been purchasing agent for Kentucky, and at the time of his appointment as comptroller, he was commissioner of finance for Kentucky. Thus he was well prepared both by training and by experience for this important position.

Mr. Peterson lost no time in completely reorganizing the financial records of the University, introducing laborsaving machines and modern methods of accounting. He established the University Stores and purchased at wholesale the products used by the University. He inventoried all the properties of the University and kept these inventories up to date. During his years of service the University has purchased some three hundred pieces of real property in its program of campus expansion, and Mr. Peterson has handled these purchases with business acumen. In his position as Vice President he has been an effective public-relations person for the University. He has been very active among the business agents of various colleges and universities, and is recognized as a leader in his profession. In recent years he has held during the summer session a school for business officers of colleges, with from fifty to seventy-five persons enrolled each year. The Vice President of Business Administration has under his direction a force of more than seven hundred persons, forming a division that is recognized as well administered.

With the establishment of the University of Kentucky Medical Center, a Vice President was urgently needed for this new organization. After considering some fifty outstanding physicians for this position, Dr. William R. Willard, dean of the medical school of Syracuse University, was selected. In the short period of his service here he has made much progress, and the new Medical Center now under construction is scheduled to open in September, 1960.

The presidency of the University of Kentucky includes approximately twenty persons who are responsible for some important aspect of the University's operation, rendering a vital service that enables the institution to function day by day. Obviously their functions cannot be set forth explicitly on these pages. There is one person in the administrative organization, however, who deserves special notice—the secretary to the President. Secretaries to college and university presidents are seldom accorded public mention for their work, but as a matter of fact, they may play a large part in the success of a president's work.

During my years as President of the University, Miss Lucy Hogan gave outstanding service as my secretary. She received graciously the visitors who came to see me. Many times she furnished them with the information they sought, or directed them to others who could answer their inquiries, thus conserving my time. She distinguished almost by instinct the callers who came on business from those who simply desired to visit. After classifying the great bulk of mail that came to my office every day, she would answer many of these letters herself, simply placing her answer on my desk for my signature. She learned my vocabulary and sentence structure so perfectly, that occasionally I did not know whether I had dictated the letter or she had written it herself. She was an encyclopedia of information about the University, with dates and places ever at hand for use.

When I had to make a trip, Miss Hogan bought my ticket, reserved a hotel room for me, furnished me with a memorandum of my business engagements, and placed all the data in a folder for my use. In preparing my calendar of engagements, she usually provided a memorandum of the information I would need in the meeting. When the general public wanted to know something about the University, they were likely to call the President, who was supposed to know everything about the University. Scores of such calls came through every day. My secretary was a genius at screening these calls, connecting me with those whose calls I should answer, and switching the other parties to the proper officials of the institution. This protection saved me much time which I could devote to more important work of the office. Thus a secretary with tact, courtesy, and intelligence can contribute greatly to the success of a president in his work. Fortunately I had such a secretary.

What are the most important activities that consume the time of a university president today? Certainly one of his chief responsibilities is to plan the program of the university. This means that he must devote many hours to quiet thought over what the university has done, what it is doing at present, and what changes should be made for the future. Much of this planning must necessarily take place in his study. There alone he will wrestle with the university's problems, and there he will try to think out a solution for them. After he has wrung from his own mind every conceivable idea, every possible procedure, he calls his trusted advisers into conference, that they may check his thinking and that together he and they may hammer out a course of action.

After a tentative program has been prepared in this way, the president will find it desirable to turn to educational literature on higher education, that he may gather ideas from others who have studied the same problem and then have published their ideas. The college president must be a constant reader of the best papers, articles, and books on college administration. He will also find it helpful to consult other presidents and deans and to exchange ideas on practices and plans before putting new programs into effect. He may learn much, too, from visits to the campuses of other educational institutions.

The president who hopes to succeed must work closely with the board of trustees. He cannot succeed unless he maintains good relations with them. The trustees of the University of

Kentucky are appointed by the governor, and over the years they have been high-class citizens with considerable interest in the University. In the years during which I have served as a college president of two different institutions, I have worked with more than fifty board members. With but one exception I have had the most cordial and happy relations with all of them.

Certainly one of the most important duties of a president is to keep his trustees informed about the institution over which he presides. He should never let a board meeting pass without giving the trustees some information about the university. It is well for him to report to them in writing such vital information as they should know. Some information should be presented informally, but in all cases he should see that it is included in the minutes of the meeting. He should secure the formal approval of all new policies and programs of the institution. Then if a difference of opinion arises afterward, the trustees will share with the president the responsibility for the action taken. Otherwise, he will have to carry the burden of responsibility alone.

A weakness of many college presidents is that they fail to keep their trustees informed about the institution. When a new member comes on the board, he should be indoctrinated regarding the duties and responsibilities of a board member. I have often requested senior trustees to talk informally to new members about the traditions, policies, and practices of the Board, and about its relation to the President and the faculty. If you find an uncooperative board member, do not try to discipline him. Rather, select one of the able trustees with seniority to work upon him and bring him into harmony with the group. I have seen this practice used with splendid results on a number of occasions.

The president must use his prerogative to present the agenda of a board meeting, and such recommendations as are to be considered by the board. Although the chairman of the board presides, it is the president's official responsibility to bring before the board the business under consideration. When this has been officially presented, it is then time for the trustees to discuss it. When the board cannot trust its president to present the business to come before the meeting, things are in a bad way.

By experience I have discovered that new trustees are likely to have distorted views of college professors. They usually respect the professor's scholarship, but they think of him as an impractical theorist who possesses little knowledge of business and what the businessman regards as the practical world. Moreover, they often regard him as a bit radical in his views on civic matters. It is an obligation of the college president to bring trustees and professors together so that they have a better understanding of one another. It is a wise president who keeps his board meetings informal and interesting, and makes sure that they do not drag out over a long period of time. A board meeting may well close with a social program. A luncheon or dinner with deans and a few professors helps to create better relations between businessmen and educators, and will send the board members home in good humor.

Long ago I discovered that a trustee could become an institution's best public-relations officer if I could get him to work on good public relations by convincing him that this was a part of his function as a trustee. It is well to honor trustees for the work they do for their institution, since their work certainly justifies recognition—and this bit of honor is about the only reward they receive for their service.

CHAPTER TWO

Financing the University Program

It is hard to say with assurance just which one of a college president's duties is his heaviest responsibility. For my part, I am inclined to say securing the funds with which to finance the institution's program, whether the institution be a college or a university, a state or a private school. Money for education is not easy to raise. No people in the world profess more insistently than Americans their faith in the value of education; but when it comes to providing funds for schools and colleges, they put a good many things ahead of education.

The most wearing part of my life as a college president was the time I spent seeking funds—even begging them, I would say—to support an institution designed to educate our own sons and daughters. The greatest sadness of my life followed a failure to secure funds to underwrite a significant program.

Securing funds with which to finance the program of the University of Kentucky has always been a difficult task for the Presidents of this institution. Through the years the University has had to operate on an inadequate budget. Too often the trustees and Presidents have had to make brick without straw. Poverty has been our lot ever since the beginning of the institution in 1865.

Table 1 in Appendix A is taken from a study prepared by Professor Ezra L Gillis entitled *The University of Kentucky, Its History and Development*. This table presents a numerical view of the growth of the University year by year from 1941 to 1956. Besides showing the increase in student enrollment, staff, volumes added to the library, and degrees awarded, it gives the increase in income from $3,370,405 in 1941 to $11,482,730 in 1956 (not including the $5,000,000 allotted by Governor A. B. Chandler to start the Medical Center). While this table seems to indicate that the amount of money received for carrying on the program of the University in 1956 was more than three times that of fifteen years earlier, this figure, of course, does not take into consideration the fact that the dollar now has only about one-half the purchasing power of the 1941 dollar.

It is important to know how the University budget is prepared in Kentucky. Every other year a new budget for the upkeep of the University is submitted to the Governor and the commissioner of finance, who then make up the State budget to be recommended to the General Assembly. It usually takes at least three months to prepare the University budget. Every departmental head, each dean of a college, and the directors of special-service departments, bureaus, and agencies participate in drawing up preliminary drafts. Their reports are finally submitted to the Vice President of Business Administration, who, with the aid of the comptroller and others, makes up the total budget, which is then presented to the President and the three Vice Presidents of the University. These administrative officials request each dean and director to meet with them and go through every item of his budget with a view to justifying it. Changes are frequently made; a request is sometimes increased, and sometimes reduced. After all these amendments in the budget are made and approved, the Vice President of Business Administration puts it into a final form for the trustees. After due consideration and approval by the trustees, it is submitted to the commissioner of finance.

In Frankfort, all too frequently in the past, our requests have been given doubtful consideration. The University has always presented an honest budget, never at any time padded. We have never sought more than we needed, as some institutions do in the hope that after a cut is made in their requests, they will still have ample funds on which to operate. During my administration two Governors, Keen Johnson (1942) and A. B. Chandler (1956), and their respective General Assemblies approved our budgetary requests without change. We trust that this precedent will be continued by future Governors and legislatures.

In my earlier years as president of a State college, I was always asked by the General Assembly's Joint Committee on Appropriations to appear before it to justify our requests for operating funds. I consider this a desirable practice, and I hope it will be renewed. This procedure would give the President an opportunity to acquaint the legislators with the justifiable needs of the University as he defends certain items in his budget.

It is important that the people of the State should become better posted on the work of their University. To meet this need, the University in recent years has prepared a biennial brochure presenting its proposed budget to the people. This is circulated among all our University alumni, State officials, members of the General Assembly, and prominent citizens of the Commonwealth. Before the distribution of the biennial brochure, a conference is held with the press and a thorough discussion of the various items presented. It is important that questions of the press should be carefully answered, for it has always given us excellent coverage. Our next move is to go to the people. The President of the University, the Vice Presidents, deans, directors, professors, and interested alumni appear before alumni associations, luncheon clubs, educational organizations, farm bureaus, labor unions, and other groups that we are able to contact, and acquaint them with the University's budget. As a result of such campaigns, the University in recent years has received more generous public support than formerly.

The financial crisis of the nation in the 1930's was a painful experience for the University of Kentucky. In 1931, when the depression had begun to deepen throughout the country, the income of the University was $2,809,584. Three years later it was down to $1,860,579, representing a loss of a million dollars per annum. Not until a decade after the crash of 1929 did the income of the University again reach that of 1931. Years passed without the restoration of professors' salaries, cut during the depression. Faculty morale was still at low ebb when I was invited to become President of the University in 1941. My first task was to secure an increase in the University's income. This was necessary primarily to restore the confidence of the faculty and other employees in the soundness and the goodwill of the University.

In this emergency Governor Keen Johnson came to our rescue. To secure an increase in financial support was no easy assignment. The State was still in debt, and Governor Johnson, though deeply interested in the University, had assured the people in his campaign that he would have a frugal administration. At first he promised the University a nominal increase in income, but this was not sufficient to relieve the crisis. Later in a lengthy conference I told the Governor about the plight of our professors because of the meager salaries they were receiving. Some people thought that professors could ease their financial strain by teaching in Summer School in addition to their regular terms of instruction. I pointed out to the Governor that only $10,000 had been appropriated by the State for Summer School, to which would be added such fees as could be collected from the summer students. These, I explained, were for the most part underpaid public-school teachers who had to attend Summer School to earn enough credits to renew an old certificate or to secure a new one. I showed the Governor, also, that fewer than half the University teachers could be employed during the summer months, and that they would receive for their summer teaching only a fraction of what they earned per month during the rest of the year. This state of affairs resulted in discontent among the professors, who felt that discrimination was being shown against them. They still remembered that in the thirties their salaries had been reduced, and that in one year during those hard times they had not received their full stipends. Moreover, there had been few promotions. Now that times were improving, it seemed to them that their position, too, should improve.

The Governor listened patiently to my long plea for more money with which to pay professors and other staff members better salaries. When I had finished, a long pause followed. Then the Governor asked what it would cost to place all University teachers on a twelve-month salary. I replied, "A 10 percent increase over the current budget (1942)." "I will recommend it to the General Assembly," responded the Governor. He also recommended $200,000 for each year of the biennium for capital improvements. The General Assembly approved these recommendations, and the University received at this session of the legislature the largest increase in its budget that it had ever had up to that time. Since that year, all permanent members of the faculty have been on a twelve-month salary. I have always considered this change an important achievement of my administration.

During the financially dark days of the early 1940's, the Haggin Trust Fund brightened an otherwise gloomy prospect. Early in 1939 President McVey had announced to the Executive Committee of the Board of Trustees that Mrs. Margaret Voorhies Haggin had created a trust fund in memory of her husband, the late James B. Haggin. Under the provisions of the trust, the University of Kentucky each year received one-half of the income available to the trust. In the history of the University, gifts have been received from time to time, but they have ordinarily been granted for some specific purpose, e.g., to aid in research in the field of agriculture, to provide equipment for improving music appreciation, or to build a Memorial Hall for the University. On the other hand, the income from the Haggin Trust Fund may be used for any purpose that the Board of Trustees designates, outside of paying for current expenses.

The income from this gift enables the institution to do many important things that a university ought to do. By means of this gift the University can look forward to a richer and more effective program through the encouragement given to the artistic and intellectual life of the institution. Over the period of eighteen years approximately one million dollars have been received from this trust. These funds have not been spent for regularly recurring expenses, but for such highly desirable equipment as a great organ that the State would not have purchased, rare books, and objects of art. This annual income from the Haggin Trust Fund has been used to finance lectureships and scholarships, the publication of scholarly books, supplementary salaries for distinguished professors, official entertainment, and a score of other desirable activities such as every institution of learning should sponsor, and such as state universities can rarely afford without receiving funds from an outside source.

The University of Kentucky will always be grateful to this farsighted woman who by her continuing memorial gift is raising the quality of the State University's cultural service to both students and faculty on the campus.

In 1942 the University of Kentucky, its President, and its professors were plunged into a serious crisis by a decision of the State Court of Appeals. The attorney general had decided upon a strict enforcement of Section 246 of Kentucky's Constitution. This Constitution of 1890 had been written by a convention of very conservative citizens who did not realize that the world in which they lived was subject to change and that the processes of civilization are dynamic. What they wrote was more than a constitution. It was actually a code of laws that were sure to become antiquated. Section 246 is a good example of the anachronisms found in this document:

No public officer, except the Governor, shall receive more than five thousand dollars per annum, as compensation for official services, independent of the compensation of legally authorized deputies and assistants, which shall be fixed and provided for by law. The

General Assembly shall provide for the enforcement of this section by suitable penalties, one of which shall be forfeiture of office by any person violating its provisions.

The President and ten deans and professors of the University of Kentucky and the president of Murray State Teachers' College were each receiving a salary in excess of $5,000 per annum, so that we were among those included in a lawsuit to determine whether we were drawing salaries in violation of the Constitution. In our case, Judge William B. Ardery of the Franklin Circuit Court held that none of the appointees of the University and Murray occupied an office created by the legislature or the Constitution. Therefore we were employees and could draw a salary in excess of $5,000 per annum. Judge Ardery, however, granted the Commonwealth of Kentucky and the commissioner of finance an appeal to the Court of Appeals of Kentucky. The real battle had just begun.

On February 24, 1942, the judges of the Court of Appeals rendered their decision, from which the following selections are made:

So far as we have been able to determine, this is the first time an employee of the state holding a position subordinate to that of an officer has tested the scope of Section 246. . . . The president and the teachers of the University of Kentucky are serving under appointment of the Board of Trustees of the University which by statute is given the power to determine the subjects to be taught; to devise the means required for instruction and admission; to appoint professors to the staff of the University; to determine and fix their salaries, duties, and official relations, and to suspend or remove them at will. . . . Applying the facts to the rule hereinabove set out, we find that by virtue of his employment each is entitled to receive fixed compensation at regular intervals; his employment is continuous; it is in the service of the public; his duties are regularly prescribed by mandate of his superiors; and, to whom he is responsible, both as to the means and methods employed in his work and as to the results obtained thereby. That being true, we are constrained to hold that the president and professors of the University and Teacher's College are employees of the state and are embraced by the provisions of Section 246 of the Constitution.

The tenor of this decision of the court was certainly derogatory as far as it applied to the presidents, deans, and professors, for it made them hirelings, lowering them in rank and degrading them in the eyes of the public. It broke the professors' spirit, making them feel that they had chosen the wrong profession and that they did not have the respect of the citizens of their State. As specific evidence of the devastating effect it had on the University, I need only point out that 12 percent of the faculty resigned in 1946, the year before this decision was reversed.

A ray of hope came from the dissenting opinion of Judge William H. Rees:

> Surely the framers of the Constitution never contemplated that the provisions of Section 246 should apply to persons employed by the state or its subdivisions to render services of an unusual or highly technical nature requiring special training and preparation. When they referred to "public officers" and "official duties" they did not have in mind school teachers, librarians, accountants, architects, engineers, and others skilled in the professions. They intended the section to apply to public officers performing the customary executive, legislative, and judicial functions of government. . . . I think Section 246 should be construed to mean exactly what it says, and should not be extended beyond the clear implication of the language employed.

Fortunately, the minority report of 1942 was destined to become the majority report of 1947.

At once reporters called on me for a statement. These are some of the things I said to them: "Naturally I am surprised and disappointed with the decision. After reading the briefs in the case, I was certain the Court of Appeals would uphold the decision of the lower court. But I am not a lawyer. . . . While we at the University of Kentucky have very few staff members receiving over $5,000 per year, nevertheless, the possibility that a faculty member could receive a higher salary stimulated the entire faculty. The loss of this stimulus is devastating. It was a goal each professor hoped some day to achieve. Now that goal is gone. . . . This decision will cause young men of genius to decline invitations to join our faculty because it will be common knowledge that there is no future advancement to be found in Kentucky comparable to that in other States. . . . This will make the University of Kentucky a training school for other universities. . . . We shall accept the decision of the Court of Appeals as good citizens. But . . . this decision erects an insurmountable hurdle and postpones the day indefinitely when the University of Kentucky can take her place alongside of the great universities of other States."

While seeking a solution to our dilemma, it occurred to me one day to turn to the Keeneland Foundation, present our urgent problem, and request aid from this organization which had always shown a genuine interest in the University. In a conference with Hal Price Headley, at that time president of the Keeneland Foundation, I presented our case, telling him of the court's decision and revealing to him the fact that most of the professors who were receiving salaries in excess of $5,000 a year were likely to leave the University. I pictured to him how disastrous this would be to our educational program. He listened patiently for ten or fifteen minutes while I pleaded that Keeneland Foundation grant the University each year a sum of money that would help to keep each professor's salary where it was at that time, the State paying $5,000 and Keeneland Foundation the remainder.

At this point Mr. Headley said, "But you know Keeneland is interested in research, especially in research on animal diseases. That is the way we want to spend our money." I responded by asking him how we could get competent researchers if we could not pay them more than $5,000. Finally Mr. Headley asked me what it would take to pay that part of the salaries in excess of the constitutional limit. I was embarrassed. I had not figured that out. I told him I would let him know soon after returning to my office. Then he said, "You win. Send me a statement at the beginning of each year of the amount it will take to keep salaries at their present level. I do not want to know the names of the people who will receive any of this money. When I get your statement, Keeneland will send you a check to cover the amount."

This generosity softened the blow which the court had dealt in 1942. The Keeneland Foundation's check continued to come annually until 1947, when the Court of Appeals reversed its previous decision and removed the $5,000 limitation on University salaries. Then we notified Keeneland that we no longer needed financial help on professors' salaries. However, generous grants have continued to come from the Keeneland Foundation for research and other projects. I personally regard Keeneland's contribution to salaries at that critical time as a gift that saved the University from educational bankruptcy.

The day after the Court of Appeals in 1942 reversed Circuit Judge Ardery's ruling that the constitutional limitation did not apply to professors' salaries, the General Assembly, on Governor Johnson's recommendation, proposed that a constitutional amendment be submitted to the voters in 1943. This amendment was designed to remove the salary limitation from the pay of technical employees, educators, engineers, and judges of the Court of Appeals. This bill passed both houses of the legislature. When it was submitted to the vote of the people in the fall of 1943, it was overwhelmingly defeated. This defeat caused further loss of faculty members and made it even more difficult to find replacements for those faculty members who had resigned.

Only those who were close to the University can fully understand how difficult it was to administer the affairs of the institution from 1942 to 1947, when prices were going up year after year and the value of the dollar was steadily going down. The University was held together largely because certain loyal members of the faculty declined to accept offers of positions in other universities or in business at salaries higher than the University could pay them.

After much deliberation I came to the conclusion that we should take the limitation-of-salary issue back to the court for another hearing. I talked informally to the Board of Trustees about it; some of the attorneys on the Board thought that a rehearing was worth trying to obtain. On my own initiative I went to Louisville to see Charles I. Dawson, a distinguished lawyer and former judge of the United States District Court for Eastern Kentucky. I reviewed for Judge Dawson the harm that had been done to the University by the 1942 decision of the Court of Appeals to limit professors' salaries to $5,000. I told him that I believed the court had erred, and that if we could get this issue before the court again, we stood a good chance of a reversal of its former decision. Then I said to Judge Dawson, "You are an alumnus of the University of Kentucky, and your children graduated from the institution. We have never before requested you to do anything for your Alma Mater, but now we need you, need you as never before. We have no money with which to pay you a fee; but we want you to take this case back to the Court and present it as only you can present it. You can win a reversal of that former decision."

The judge was silent for a long time—at least a minute, possibly two. Then he said, "I am not in the habit of practicing law for the fun of it; but I am going to take your case and I am going to win it."

Some weeks later the case was presented to the Franklin Circuit Court under the title, *Pardue et al. v. Miller, Commissioner of Finance*. The circuit judge upheld the decision of the Court of Appeals in 1942 that the limitations in Section 246 did apply to employees. The suit was then taken to the Kentucky Court of Appeals. All members of the higher court were present when Judge Dawson presented his case. I was one of six or eight persons present in the courtroom when this master of logic gave his argument. Those present were profoundly impressed. I was certain that he had won his case long before the court rendered its decision. Charles I. Dawson should always be remembered as one of the great benefactors of the University of Kentucky.

The opinion of the Court was written by Commissioner O. W. Stanley. All but two members of the court concurred. Judge Stanley said in part:

> Our opinion was that the presidents and professors of the University and the Teachers Colleges are employees and not public officers of the state, although at first blush it would appear that one holding a place so exalted and responsible is an officer. Our classification is in accord with the decisions of other courts. Thus, in Martin v. Smith, 239 Wis. 214 . . . it was held in a well reasoned opinion that the president of the University of Wisconsin is not a public officer of the state within the meaning of the section of the Constitution of Wisconsin. . . . In enumerating the characteristic elements of public office, the court noted, among other things, that the president of the University did not exercise any part of the sovereign power of the state, but that, instead, such power was exercised by the university's board of regents, the president merely having power to manage and direct the university and carry out its policies and duties as set forth by the board of regents. . . .
>
> As in the construction of statutes, the courts often search for an intention respecting a given fact or condition when in truth the members of the legislature, or, as in this case, the framers of the constitution and the people adopting it, never had any intention concerning that fact or condition. . . . We ought not to attribute an intention where there was none. . . .
>
> Our conclusion is that Section 246 of the Constitution is to be construed and applied as written. And it does not include a professor of the University of Kentucky. Therefore, we overrule so much of the opinion in Talbott v. Public Service Commission of Kentucky, 291 Ky. 109, . . . as is in conflict with this decision. The judgment is reversed for the entry of one consistent with this opinion.

It was not until 1949 that the General Assembly again presented to a vote of the people an amendment of Section 246 of the Constitution. This time a real campaign was carried on, and at last it was carried, though not by an overwhelming vote.

While in our struggle over Section 246 I never lost confidence that we would finally win, I was deeply grieved to see the

University stymied in its progressive work for the State. One after another, scholarly, dynamic, and personable young professors left us to go to other universities because we could not pay them a fitting salary. I shall never forget how I suffered in the flesh during those years of heartrending experience. In the fifteen years of my presidency this experience stands out as my "crisis extraordinary."

CHAPTER THREE

Emergency Building for a University

THE fifteen years between 1941 and 1956 were years of emergency building for the University of Kentucky as well as for many another university in the United States. Table 2 in Appendix A lists the buildings constructed on the University of Kentucky campus in this period, giving name and use of each building, date of construction, and cost. A study of this table shows that from the standpoint of construction these buildings fall into three distinct groups, each characterized by its own type of emergency.

While the total number of buildings in this list is 36, it is noteworthy that only three of these buildings were built in the war years 1941-1945, two of these being research laboratories and one a building for physical education. The cost of these three buildings amounted to only $168,400. With labor and building materials needed for war uses, the University almost ceased to build.

The second period, 1946-1947, shows considerable construction on the campus, but of an unusual character. Returning veterans in great numbers created new needs. Of the fifteen buildings built in this emergency period, twelve are listed as temporary, and most of them were for housing or for classroom-laboratory use. Eight of the fifteen buildings cost less than $50,000 apiece.

In the third period, 1948-1956, the stage of temporary build-

EMERGENCY BUILDING FOR A UNIVERSITY

ing was over. Of the eighteen buildings and building groups listed for these years, none was temporary. Seven cost more than a million dollars each, and four others cost more than half a million. Eight of the eighteen were dormitories. This rapid building of large dormitories reveals the postwar pressure for living quarters.

While the total cost of University building between 1941 and 1956 amounted to about 20.7 million dollars, 10.9 million dollars of this total was spent for housing projects, of which 10.0 million dollars' worth were permanent structures. The next few years of campus building, too, must necessarily be in a certain sense emergency construction, though permanent. The pressing need for housing has unavoidably restricted other types of building. As a result, the University is now in desperate need of eight or ten new classroom buildings and a large addition to its library.

The rapid growth in the value of the University's plant merits some attention. On July 1, 1941, the appraised value of the plant was $8,333,405. In 1956 the total value of the fixed assets as appraised by the Industrial Appraisal Company of Pittsburgh was $41,094,791. In this fifteen-year span, the assets of the institution had increased approximately fivefold. Or one may observe the increase in assets from another angle. The value of the fixed assets of the University at the close of its seventy-sixth year (1941) was about 8.3 million dollars. Fifteen years later its fixed assets showed an increase of 32.7 million dollars to the total of 41.0 million dollars in 1956. Another illustration of the University's growth in operating plant is shown in the following comparison: President McVey in his report for the biennium 1935-1937 said that in the 72-year period from 1865 to 1937, the total amount of money voted by the legislature for construction of buildings was $1,234,000. Table 2 shows that in the fifteen-year period from 1941 to 1956, the total amount spent for buildings was $20,730,922, though only about one-fifth of this amount was voted by the legislature.

Kentucky has always been rather sparing in its expenditure

for classroom buildings, libraries, and laboratories. It was comparatively easy to secure funds for a fieldhouse and for the enlargement of the stadium. During the fifteen years when I was President, the only permanent classroom building erected out of State appropriations was the Fine Arts Building, costing $1,646,966. The other buildings erected during the last decade and a half have been paid for largely by means of revenue bonds issued by the Board of Trustees, to be redeemed over a period of from 20 to 40 years. These buildings are being erected, one might say, out of money coming from the parents of the students who attend the University of Kentucky. They have been erected by the same method that is used when the State constructs a toll road or a toll bridge. The users—in this case the students who attend the University—pay the toll on these University buildings. I am always surprised when I hear taxpayers claiming credit for some new dormitory in which there may not be a dollar of tax money.

During the fifteen years of my administration as President of the University, the State has appropriated $5,901,206 for buildings and other capital improvements for the University, while the trustees through a bond plan have issued $7,907,500 in revenue bonds for capital improvements. The Federal government spent at least $2,000,000 on veteran housing. The remainder of the money for campus building was provided by individuals, frequently alumni, and by groups, such as the Keeneland Foundation.

The University's experience with veterans' housing has formed an interesting part of the institution's history. At the close of World War II a challenging problem faced the colleges and universities of the nation, namely, how to house the thousands of young veterans returning to college under the provisions of the G. I. Bill of Rights, enacted by Congress on recommendation of President Franklin D. Roosevelt.

The University of Kentucky was one of the first institutions to establish housing projects for veterans after the close of hostilities in August, 1945. The University had literally thousands of applications from veterans returning from war. Probably half of them had young wives, and many had one or two children. We had no housing for married students when the war was over. Out of Washington came an announcement that the Federal government would help the colleges and universities by giving them surplus housing available in army camps and at the location of federally operated plants.

I consulted Colonel James H. Graham, dean of the College of Engineering, at that time consultant to the Secretary of War, about the possibility of the University's securing some of this surplus housing. When he came to Lexington on business about this time, we discussed college housing for married veterans at great length. While returning to Washington by train, he passed through Charlestown, Indiana, and from the train he saw hundreds of new prefabricated houses that had just been completed for use of the workers in the powder plant there. In Washington he took up this matter with the proper authorities, and was assured that the University could have these houses already furnished for the nominal sum of $5 per house, but that we would have to move them from Charlestown, Indiana, to Lexington. These houses were transferred by trucks in the early fall of 1945—200 from Charlestown and 124 from Willow Run, Michigan. It became necessary for the University to construct sewers, streets, and electric lines. Thus within a few months a veterans' village, Cooperstown, came into existence. At its maximum its 324 veterans and their families constituted a population of nearly 1,000, more than many a county-seat town in Kentucky.

When Cooperstown was completed, we applied to the Federal Public Housing Authority for another housing project for veterans, Shawneetown. This village had 182 housing units. The construction of this project progressed very slowly, and the cost appeared to us to be abnormally high. Since it was being paid for by Federal authorities, however, the University had no control over its cost.

The University requested the two veterans' villages to set up their own form of government. Each village was presided over by a mayor and a council elected by the veterans. All problems relative to the government of these two communities were resolved by the veterans themselves. This represented one of the most interesting experiments that I have ever seen. As an example of the community problems which were solved by this village government, I recall that on one occasion about a year after Cooperstown had been opened, the mayor called at my office to talk over a problem that seriously disturbed him and the other members of the village council, the matter of whether the residents of Cooperstown could or could not own dogs.

It appeared from his story that the young families with little children did not want dogs running around the closely built village because a mother then could not leave a baby alone in its carriage outdoors. On the other hand, many young couples without children insisted upon their reasonable right to have dogs in their household. The mayor said that the council was equally divided over this question and could not arrive at a conclusion. This was the first issue on which they had not been able to make a ready adjustment. The young mayor asked me as President to write him a note saying that the administration of the University of Kentucky was outlawing dogs in Cooperstown and that all residents of the village must get rid of their dogs by the opening of school the following September. By this means the President could solve a very controversial issue for the community.

I listened to the story. Presently I said, "I can do that for you. However, I was under the impression that it was some such situation as this that caused you to go to war and spend two or three years of your life fighting over how public questions should be resolved. Do you want me to be a dictator, or do you want to solve this issue by the democratic process?" The young man had been listening very carefully. "I get your point," he said. "We'll handle this problem ourselves." He shook my hand warmly and left.

The Federal Public Housing Authority also erected on our

campus barracks that housed 488 single veterans. These were temporary living quarters that were not very satisfactory. However, they made it possible for a number of veterans to attend the University who could not have had this opportunity had the barracks not been constructed.

About the same time by an Act of Congress the Federal government provided us with a number of temporary service buildings. Among these were a large classroom building, a chemistry laboratory, a storage annex, an engineering laboratory, a small building for dramatic and speech classes, a shop, and a cafeteria. As these structures are of a temporary nature, they should be removed from the campus as soon as permanent buildings can be erected. In the construction of these buildings the Federal government has spent at least $2,000,000. The State of Kentucky did not contribute to the erection of these temporary projects.

When the Federal government gave the University the prefabricated houses and barracks to house veterans and their families, it was with the understanding that they were to be dismantled after five years. This period stretched out to ten years, and these buildings had disintegrated to such an extent that they became in appearance the slums of Lexington and wholly unfit for housing. Time and again we requested the State government to appropriate funds for dormitories for young men and women, and apartments for married students. We received only a token appropriation on one dormitory, and all other requests were denied. Kentucky during its entire history has erected at the State's expense only one dormitory, Patterson Hall, built in 1905 at the cost of $10,500. The trustees after much study decided to embark upon a building program to erect permanent buildings for students wishing to attend the University, but who could not find living quarters. Applications were made to the Public Housing Administration for loans; these were approved, and revenue bonds were issued for the construction of Bowman Hall, Keeneland Hall, Holmes Hall, Donovan Hall, six small dormitories for men, and Cooperstown and Shawneetown apartments for married students. Most of these projects have been completed and are in use.

In 1950 a large Service Building was opened, and space was found here for storage of considerable library material and duplicating apparatus used by the library. In 1951 a well-equipped building for the School of Journalism was opened, the Enoch Grehan Journalism Building, which met a very pressing need.

When I was first appointed President of the University, I discovered that the general public had been demanding a fieldhouse on the University campus large enough to accommodate the many thousands of citizens as well as the students who demanded admission to the basketball games. The Alumni Gymnasium would hold only about one-half of the student body. The citizens of the State who wished to see the basketball games had to travel to Louisville or New York to witness the playing of the fabulous team we had at that time. Personally I did not think that a fieldhouse was the first and greatest building need of the University. However, it was on the agenda as the first need so far as the citizens of the State were concerned, and it would have been futile for us to place any other building ahead of it.

In the first address I made after my appointment as President, I said to the Alumni Association at their banquet, June 5, 1941: "I shall recommend to the trustees for their approval a request to the Governor and the next General Assembly for an appropriation for a building that will properly take care of athletics, our health service, physical education, and recreation. For the construction of this building we shall ask for a sum of money that will be equivalent to the cost of one of the nation's first class bombers. . . . I do not believe this is an unreasonable request."

I strove to change the type of building which had been considered by many friends of the University. Instead of making it primarily a gymnasium, we had the architects design a building to be used both as an auditorium and as a center for basketball. The Coliseum was not to be a building solely for athletics, but rather an all-University building where any program for the cultural, civic, educational, recreational, and spiritual development of our students could be held, when the attendance at these programs could not be accommodated in our small auditoriums on the campus. As an auditorium it would seat approximately 15,000 people, and when used as a gymnasium, 11,000, with standing room for 1,000 additional.

Nine years intervened between my original recommendation and the dedication of the Memorial Coliseum. We had to clear the slum area covering two and three-tenths acres where the building was to be located. This was one of the most difficult tasks that the administrators of the University had ever tackled. However, we had the cooperation of many splendid citizens of Lexington and of Fayette County. Appropriations for the Coliseum from the State amounted to $3,100,000, made under the administrations of Governors Keen Johnson, Simeon Willis, and Earle Clements, and by the General Assemblies of 1942, 1946, and 1948. As the State appropriations were not sufficient to complete the building as planned, the Board of Trustees sold $825,000 worth of bonds to finish it. These bonds are being liquidated over a period of twenty years out of income from athletic events held on the campus. The total cost of the Coliseum was approximately $4,000,000, of which the taxpayers invested $3,100,000.

The University convocations and commencements are held regularly in the Memorial Coliseum. The joint programs of the Central Kentucky Community Concert Association, the Lexington Public Forum, and the University of Kentucky are regularly scheduled events held in this building. Some of the world's greatest musicians and lecturers have appeared on these programs. The joint association is the largest of its kind in the United States. It is composed of a membership of more than 6,000 citizens and about 8,000 students, who each year have the chance to hear from eleven to twelve great programs. On these programs have been such orchestral groups as the London

Royal Philharmonic Orchestra, Sir Thomas Beecham conducting, the Cleveland Symphony Orchestra, the Danish State Orchestra, the Pittsburgh Symphony Orchestra with Nathan Milstein as violinist, and the New York Symphony. Among individual artists have been heard James Melton, Roberta Peters, Marian Anderson, Artur Rubenstein, Dorothy Kirsten, Lily Pons, Jascha Heifetz, and Gina Bachauer. Among first-rank speakers have appeared Senator Margaret Chase Smith, Elmer Davis, Charles Laughton, Eric Severeid, the Honorable Herbert Morrison, and Basil Rathbone.

The number of people attending cultural, educational, and recreational programs in the Coliseum exceeds the number who have attended athletic events. While not the largest building of its kind in the United States, it is regarded as one of the best combinations of auditorium and gymnasium in this or any other country.

On the walls along the ramps of Memorial Coliseum are inscribed the names of 9,265 Kentuckians who lost their lives in World War II, and also the names of about 1,000 other Kentuckians who died in the Korean War. Attached to the walls in the concourse are bronze stars bearing the names of 334 University men who lost their .lives in World War II. This structure will stand endlessly as a valued memorial to those who died in the hope that the dignity of the individual might not perish from the earth. They exchanged their youth for an ideal that is both noble and enduring.

CHAPTER FOUR

Relations with Faculty and Staff

ONE major activity of the university president is working with his faculty. Many presidents delegate this function to the deans and heads of departments. I admit that in larger institutions most of this work will have to be done by deans and vice presidents. Nevertheless, I am convinced that the door to the president's office should never be closed to a professor. In my own experience I have seen professors rejuvenated in their professional growth as the result of an occasional conference with the president. When these professors realized that the president knew something about their work and that he had a genuine interest in it, they appeared to draw new strength from this stimulus. During my years as a college president I have always managed to keep a considerable block of my time open to conference with professors. It is time well spent, and I believe I gained as much value out of these conferences as did the professors. Now that I think over my years as a president, I would not for anything have missed this experience.

A high degree of understanding and cordiality should flow from the office of the presidency—including all persons connected with the office—toward the faculty and staff. Be not too sparing of praise. Compliment good work and recognize achievement. Be ready to encourage a struggling instructor. A little praise sometimes means more than an increase in salary —but give both whenever possible. In building up a great institution, no single thing that a president can do is more important than to maintain a high morale in the faculty and staff. After his retirement President Arthur Hadley, for twenty-two years at Yale, declared that the most exhausting task of a university president was that of helping his faculty members to pull together instead of separately. Henry Noble MacCracken, for many years president of Vassar College, remarked, "I never succeeded in eliminating faculty tensions. Some folks just do not like others." Our campus philosopher Ezra L Gillis, himself a professor for half a century, has said that if he could invent a salve that would take the soreness out of professors, he would endow the University. As I look back upon my experience as a college president, I recognize the truth in what these elder educational statesmen have said. It takes much time and diplomacy to keep a faculty working together; but without teamwork, no institution can make much progress.

Here at the University of Kentucky we have had our full share of faculty feuds. Back in the old days when we were the Agriculture and Mechanical College of the denominational Kentucky University (1865-1878), there was feuding between the scientists and the theologians on the subject of evolution. President H. S. Barker had feuding in the faculty among the separate engineering colleges, and this fight eventually resulted in his resigning the presidency. The most unpleasant misunderstanding within the faculties during the McVey administration was a controversy between the College of Engineering and the College of Arts and Sciences over matters relating to curricula. During my fifteen years at the University I have certainly had my share of faculty feuds, in spite of the effort I have made personally to keep peace in the academic family. One of the unhappiest quarrels during my administration took place in the Department of Agronomy. Capable scientists, well-educated men, fell out over the relative merits of fescue and other grasses. A bitter and lasting hostility developed between these professors who had previously been colleagues and friends. Dean Cooper and I tried to conciliate these men, all of whom we respected, but it could not be done. I eventually discovered that fescue was only an excuse for this hostility; the real cause was professional jealousy. One of these professors was a very congenial, personable, and attractive man who spoke convincingly to farmers on agricultural subjects. After a farm conference adjourned, farmers frequently gathered around him and generously handed out compliments. This annoyed some of his colleagues. When I became convinced that this was the cause of the trouble, I moved in on these feudists. Eventually what I had to do to stop the quarrel was to accept the resignation of the head of the department, retire another professor, and find a position in another institution for a capable and distinguished man in the department. I let it be known, too, that other persons active in the altercation would be removed unless the quarreling ceased. It took about two years to restore harmony. The scars resulting from this feud will never be wholly forgotten by some of the participants.

All too often an antagonistic attitude grows up between the president and his professors. It is a little hard to understand why this springs up. Nearly always the new president is a former professor and colleague. Being made president should not change his nature or behavior. But most college presidents, as soon as they are installed, have experienced an aloofness on the part of their former colleagues. I do not believe that I changed when I was appointed a college president almost thirty years ago. I am sure that I did not have a superior feeling as the result of my appointment; in fact, it humbled me. No one that I know of has ever charged me with being a czar or a dictator. I have constantly striven to develop democratic policies in the two institutions in which I have served as president. Never have I vetoed an action of the faculty, although I have opposed a few of their decisions. When the faculty, which I have regarded as comprising the legislative body of the University, have adopted a policy, I have enforced it even when I doubted its wisdom.

When any disagreement has arisen between the Board of

Trustees and the faculty or any individual professor—and such disagreements have come up—I have stood by the faculty. I have felt that this was my duty. Through the years I have spent much of my time and energy endeavoring to improve the status of the faculty. I have begged Governors and legislators for more money to pay better salaries to our teachers and other staff members. On more than one occasion I have declined to accept an increase in salary which the Board wanted to give me, because I believed the professors and other employees were underpaid.

Always as President I have considered myself in the service of the faculty. I have sought more pay for them, a better library for their use and the use of their students, the best scientific equipment for their laboratories, more space for their departments, and a more inviting atmosphere in which to live and work. It is the faculty that make a great university.

While the curriculum of a college or university is largely determined by the faculty, the president has some responsibility to warn them against the danger of overexpansion of courses. I have often said to our faculty that they keep their salaries down by continually increasing the number of courses offered in their departments. This results in the demand for another professor or two in the department, and this multiplication of courses results in smaller classes. Each new instructor has some "pet" course that he wants added to the curriculum. Year after year this process goes on, with seldom a suggestion that a course be dropped. The initiative should be taken by professors to bring about some order in the chaos now prevailing. A president who would arbitrarily remove courses from the catalog offerings would be termed a dictator, but responsible faculty should be encouraged to study this trend and bring about a more rational program of course offerings.

From its earliest years the University of Kentucky has had some distinguished scholars and excellent teachers. However, throughout its history the University's budget has been too limited to permit it to hold the teachers who have been enticed

RELATIONS WITH FACULTY AND STAFF 41

away by other institutions offering larger salaries. A long roster could be made of the talented teachers who began their careers here and then left to receive better salaries elsewhere. Many of these gifted young professors have become distinguished scholars and have brought fame to other institutions of higher education. The better salaries now paid its faculty by the University of Kentucky have gone a long way in correcting this situation. Table 3 in Appendix A compares the salaries of various ranks of teachers in the University in 1940-1941 with the salaries of the same ranking teachers in the University in 1946-1947 and in 1956-1957.

When I came to the presidency of the University of Kentucky, the deans depended largely on correspondence and letters of reference when about to employ new faculty members, as there were no funds provided for the traveling expenses of prospective teachers. I promptly requested the trustees to permit me to spend out of the Haggin Fund, over which the State had no control, the expenses of any candidate invited for an interview for a position of relatively high rank. We asked the deans and heads of departments to invite at least three candidates for each vacancy, and the University paid the traveling expenses for all of them.

When these persons came to the campus, they were interviewed by the head of the department and some of the professors in the department, the dean of the college, the Vice President of the University, and the President. Instead of having a selection made by one or two people, a group judgment was obtained. I am satisfied that this plan of recruiting new teachers has resulted in our securing far better personnel than we obtained by the old method. The financial cost has been insignificant as compared with our gain in quality of personnel. Often when we were about to fill a very important vacancy, we have invited some professor to visit our institution to deliver a lecture or a series of lectures, or to conduct a seminar.

Our new plan of granting leaves of absence on pay has also raised the quality of our young professors. These grants have assisted many a young professor in completing a research project which he might never have finished without some such financial aid. Such timely cooperation of his University in his scholarly pursuits increases his morale and his devotion to the institution.

The University has stimulated many professors by setting aside funds for defraying the expenses of faculty members to attend scientific and professional meetings. It has aided many of the faculty in securing fellowships and grants from foundations for study abroad. It has been generous in granting leaves of absence to professors who have desired to accept government assignments in this country and abroad to do certain technical and scientific work that they were especially well qualified to perform. Since the close of World War II, we have had University of Kentucky professors studying, teaching, and rendering technical services in Great Britain, France, Spain, Switzerland, Italy, Germany, Austria, Norway, Sweden, Holland, Japan, Greece, India, Indonesia, Egypt, Pakistan, Mexico, Central America, Venezuela, New Zealand, and other countries. These experiences have greatly stimulated our professors, given them a broader perspective, increased their knowledge of peoples and countries, and made them more interesting teachers than they could possibly have been without such contacts.

In recent years all appointees to the faculty of the University have been required to hold a doctor's degree before they can attain permanent tenure on the staff. Professors and associate professors must have the doctorate when they are employed. An instructor is not ordinarily retained if he does not merit promotion in five years. This emphasis on scholarship has done much to upgrade our faculty in recent years. On the whole, the faculty is a society of scholars in the pursuit of knowledge. Approximately ninety persons of our staff are in *Who's Who in America*. The University of Kentucky is a center of culture where scholarly books are written, where scholarly research is pursued, and where the results are published in books, journals, and magazines.

RELATIONS WITH FACULTY AND STAFF

About a decade ago the University established ten Distinguished Professorships. These positions are awarded to professors only. They have been given with great care, and at no time have all the positions been filled. They are granted in recognition of notable service to the University in either teaching or research, and in recognition of outstanding scholarship or creative ability in a particular field. The title carries with it a salary increment and certain privileges. There has also been established an additional title of "Distinguished Professor of the Year in Arts and Sciences," awarded annually to a professor in the College of Arts and Sciences by secret ballot of the faculty. These Distinguished Professorships carry decided prestige, and as a result they are highly regarded by members of the faculty. This policy has resulted in stimulating a greater interest in teaching, research, and creative scholarship on the part of our more ambitious professors.

When a vacancy occurred in the deanship of a college, it was our policy to address a letter to each member of the faculty of the college having the rank of professor, associate professor, or assistant professor, asking his views on a man to fill the vacancy. We asked him to recommend three persons as candidates in order of preference from our own staff and a like number from outside the University. Each faculty member was asked to write to the President freely expressing his views, or if he preferred, to come to the President's office. This request usually brought a high percentage of response from the faculty.

In 1951 there was a catch in this procedure. We were seeking a candidate to replace the retiring Thomas P. Cooper as dean of the College of Agriculture and Home Economics, director of the Agricultural Experiment Station, and director of Agricultural Extension—a very responsible position. I went through the customary preliminaries of seeking the opinion of the faculty and staff concerned. Soon it developed that there were certain political interests in the State that apparently wished to take this appointment out of the hands of the President. I had been unaware of this move until action was started at a meeting of the Board of Trustees. Just as the Board was about to adjourn, one member arose and said it was a known fact that Dean Cooper was about to retire, and therefore he moved that the chairman appoint a committee to consider the matter and bring a recommendation to the Board for its consideration. At once I was on my feet. I pointed out calmly to the trustees that the laws relating to the University gave the President the authority to nominate all employees and that no appointment could be made until he had made such a nomination. Then I pointed out with great deliberation that if the Board had lost confidence in me and believed that I was not competent to bring to them a good recommendation, they should appoint a committee to select a new President. Then I sat down, and there was a long pause. The motion died for want of a second.

While this matter was being agitated, Allan M. Trout of the Louisville *Courier-Journal* interviewed me on the matter of the appointment of a new dean. This gave me an opportunity to get before the people the kind of man we were seeking and the qualifications we would expect the next dean to have. Mr. Trout's article of January 5, 1951, ran as follows: "Dr. H. L. Donovan, president of the University of Kentucky, is engaged in one of the biggest man hunts of his career. He's looking for a successor to Dr. Thomas P. Cooper, dean of the College of Agriculture since 1918.... If Dr. Donovan reduced his requirements to an advertisement, this is about how the ad would read: 'Wanted: A dean for the College of Agriculture at the University of Kentucky. Must be a man in his early 40's, with high courage, unquestioned integrity, and the ability to get along with people. Must have been reared on a farm and now possess a Ph.D. degree in agriculture. Must have a pleasing personality, plus the ability to speak with equal assurance and clarity to a group of farmers, a committee of Congress, or a forum of agriculture scientists. Must be ready to assume duties July 1, 1951.'"

I have always felt deeply grateful to Mr. Trout for the article.

Many of the other Kentucky papers also took up the subject, and soon there was a climate of opinion thoroughly in accord with the manner in which we pursued our search for a dean.

I am opposed to letting the head of a department select the members of his department alone. I am opposed to permitting a dean to fill vacancies on his own judgment. I am opposed to a president acting without advice from his colleagues in employing administration officials. For the best results in the selection of a faculty and a staff, the composite judgment of a number of qualified persons will be superior to any single judgment. While President of the University, I insisted that all vacancies be filled on the basis of a group judgment of responsible members of the faculty and staff. This, I believe, is one reason why the University has an outstanding faculty today.

During the fifteen years I was at the University, not a single position was filled on any basis but that of merit. Though there were occasions when political pressure was attempted, it never succeeded.

The most important factor in the building of a great university is the professor. He is more important than fine buildings and beautiful grounds—even more important than a good library and excellent laboratories, essential as these are. As the professors are, so is the university.

When I arrived at the University of Kentucky on July 1, 1941, I found many a teacher living on the borderline of poverty. The depression of the 1930's had reduced their standard of living for nearly a decade. Few of them had received increases in salary, though the cost of living had been gradually rising. My first objective was to raise the economic status of the professor. I never ceased to work on this problem. Table 3 in Appendix A shows to what extent we succeeded over the years in improving the faculty salaries during this period. Though we were never fully satisfied with the result, we never stopped trying.

CHAPTER FIVE

New Colleges and Departments

THE years of my administration, especially after the close of World War II, were times of great expansion in the University. The faculty and the staff doubled in numbers in these years. Practically every department added new professors in its expanding program to provide for a student body that had more than doubled.

During the war we spent all new income in attempting to strengthen the old, established colleges and departments rather than to create new colleges and departments. While there was constant pressure on the administration to extend its services into new fields, the trustees and faculty supported us in the position we had taken in regard to this matter.

Near the close of the war, when our financial status had improved somewhat, we recommended that a Department of Geography be established in the College of Arts and Sciences (1944). This recommendation was approved by the trustees, and the department was organized. It has enrolled hundreds of students and has already made a distinct contribution in this field of learning so long neglected in Kentucky.

Shortly after the close of hostilities, Dean Earl Slone, heading a committee of trustees and faculty from the College of Pharmacy, an independent institution in Louisville, called upon us and presented a proposal that this College of Pharmacy become a college of the University of Kentucky. This committee agreed that they were ready to turn over all their properties and endowment to the University of Kentucky if they could be integrated into the University. At first we were hesitant about a merger of this kind; but after numerous conferences between the administrative officials of the University of Kentucky and the dean and trustees of the College of Pharmacy of Louisville, our Board of Trustees approved the consolidation of the two institutions.

One provision of the agreement was that the College of Pharmacy would be moved to the Lexington campus as soon as a new building could be provided. At that time we thought that an appropriation could be secured for this college in a year or two; yet in spite of the fact that practically all the druggists of Kentucky were exerting their influence to get an appropriation from the State, eight years passed before the Building Commission approved the request. In 1955 the Commonwealth of Kentucky allotted $475,500 for this project, and the University from funds received from the trustees of the College of Pharmacy appropriated $161,382 for the same purpose. An attractive building costing $636,882 was completed by September, 1957, in time for the College of Pharmacy to move to Lexington for the opening of school.

This college has proved to be a great asset to the State of Kentucky. It graduates from 40 to 50 pharmacists each year to fill the demands of the druggists of the State. An able faculty has been assembled to teach Kentucky students who are interested in careers as pharmacists. This college will also make a real contribution to the new Medical Center now being constructed at the University of Kentucky.

Out of accumulated funds from the Campus Book Store and profits from the Kernel Press, the trustees erected the Enoch Grehan Journalism Building in 1951. After making a thorough study of the Department of Journalism, it was decided to make it a School of Journalism. A beautifully designed building was constructed, costing more than three-quarters of a million dollars, new presses and other essential equipment were installed, and additional personnel were appointed to the new School of Journalism. These facilities have helped to make this school one of the nation's outstanding institutions for the education of journalists. Partly as a result of these improvements, it has enrolled many students from other states. Soon after World War II, ten able young journalists from Germany came to the United States under the sponsorship of the United States government for the purpose of studying journalism in this country. They were sent to Lexington and enrolled in our School of Journalism. Since then, many journalists from other countries have also enrolled here.

In order to give greater prestige to the Department of Home Economics of the College of Agriculture and Home Economics, we recommended that it be made a School of Home Economics. The Board of Trustees concurred in this recommendation. A new building for this school was built and equipped with the latest facilities available. Also, additional staff was employed for the new School of Home Economics.

Two other expansions have been initiated recently through the cooperation of certain colleges of the University. The College of Arts and Sciences and the College of Engineering have planned a curriculum for the training of chemical engineers. The College of Engineering and the College of Agriculture have initiated a course for the preparation of agricultural engineers. Students preparing for chemical engineering and agricultural engineering are enrolled in both colleges, and their degrees are conferred jointly by the two cooperating colleges.

During the earlier years of Dr. McVey's administration, the Department of Extension Education was established. Extension classes were set up largely for teachers who were improving their training. Professors from the campus taught these courses. The subjects taught were mainly in the fields of literature, history, political science, geography, and education. Very few courses in science were offered, since these branches required laboratories for effective teaching. There was seldom a request for courses in mathematics and the foreign languages. The area served was within a radius of about 100 miles from Lexington, though some classes were organized in towns as far away from Lexington as 150 miles. There was always a great demand for correspondence courses, and literally thousands of ambitious students who desired to learn while working carried on correspondence study. The department expanded its service from time to time. It set up a library of teaching films and other visual aids, which were made available to schools, clubs, and colleges over the State.

In January, 1948, I proposed to the Board of Trustees the establishment of a University Extension Center at Covington, Kentucky, under the supervision of the Department of Extension Education. I pointed out in my recommendation that Northern Kentucky, as represented by the counties of Boone, Campbell, and Kenton, had a population of 175,877, according to the 1940 census. This was only a little less than the population of Fayette and the six adjoining counties served by our extension service.

The University enrollment from the Northern Kentucky counties in the fall of 1947 was 333, whereas 2,203 students were enrolled from Fayette and the six adjoining counties. Only one senior college, Villa Madonna, was located in the Northern Kentucky area, while in Fayette and the surrounding counties there were six senior colleges in addition to the University. It was apparent that a very small percentage of high-school graduates were attending college. On the basis of these facts, a University Center in Covington, if properly organized, would serve a large number of youths of college age. I stated, too, that a University of Kentucky Center in Covington would serve business and professional groups with informal educational activities. This center would assist greatly in making Northern Kentucky a real part of the University campus.

I also emphasized to the Board of Trustees that a number of veterans who wanted to continue their education would be attracted to the center if we offered courses in which they were interested. Courses offered in Covington would help to ease the veterans' housing problem on the Lexington campus. I showed also that in establishing such a center in Covington, we would be doing what neighboring state universities were doing, such as those of Illinois, Indiana, Virginia, Alabama, and Tennessee. The Board took my recommendation under consideration, and after thoroughly discussing it, directed the President to put it into operation. This was the beginning of the University Extension Center in Covington, Kentucky.

With the passing of years, the Department of Extension Education grew rapidly in its service to the people. Then I became convinced that the department should be expanded and the program dignified by placing it on the basis of a college. Therefore, on June 1, 1954, I recommended the establishment of a College of Adult and Extension Education of the University of Kentucky, making this college responsible for all adult-education activities of the University. This college was to be administered by a dean as other colleges of the University are administered. It should be the business of this college to carry the services of the entire University (except in the areas of agriculture and home economics) to the people of the State in whatever ways might seem desirable and feasible. Such programs as night schools, institutes, short courses, clinics, conferences, and other special programs, whether offered with or without credit, should be under the direction of this new college. When my recommendation had been approved by the Board of Trustees, I promptly asked the Board to appoint Dr. Lyman V. Ginger as the dean of this college. His appointment became effective July 1, 1954.

While Horace Holley was president of Transylvania University (1817-1827), Lexington was regarded as one of the foremost medical centers in the United States. He employed on the faculty of the Medical School such distinguished physicians of that day as Dr. Daniel Drake, professor of materia medica and medical botany, Dr. Benjamin Dudley, professor of anatomy and surgery, and Dr. William Richardson, professor of chemistry. Under the leadership of President Holley they assembled one of the best medical libraries in the country. This Medical School had at one time the largest attendance of any medical school in the United States with the single exception of the Medical College at Philadelphia.

In 1837 an effort was made to have the Transylvania Medical School moved to Louisville. Though this was not successful, the discussion led to a bitter quarrel among physicians, and eventually led to a decline in the Transylvania Medical School. Finally it had to suspend operation because its building and equipment were destroyed by fire in 1863, thus ending a half century of progress in medical education in Lexington.

I find no evidence that either President Patterson (1869-1910) or President Barker (1910-1916) considered seriously the establishment of a medical school at the University of Kentucky. The late President McVey frequently discussed with me the desirability of founding a school of medicine at the University, but he said that he had never recommended it because the existing colleges were so poorly financed. He feared that they would be further impoverished if a college of medicine were established.

After I became President of the University of Kentucky, it was a common thing for State senators and representatives attending a session of the General Assembly at Frankfort to come to Lexington and call on me informally about the prospect of establishing a medical school at the University. Sometimes they would already have a bill prepared, calling for the appropriation of one or two million dollars for this purpose. When I would tell them about what a medical school costs, they would lose their enthusiasm for the project. These callers were always from the rural areas or the mountain counties where there were but few doctors available for medical service.

In the early part of my administration, I took the same position on this question as President McVey had taken. I was afraid that a medical school would handicap the existing colleges, since they were operating on budgets far too small for high-grade teaching. I opposed the establishment of a new medical school until a time when the State would support more generously the colleges already in existence. After the close of World War II, Kentucky people became even more concerned about the State's inadequate medical service, especially in rural areas. There was a growing conviction that there were too few physicians in Kentucky and that the State should assume its proper responsibility in providing medical service for the people. The rural press became vocal on the subject, and many editorials demanded action on the part of the legislature.

At a meeting of the General Assembly in 1948, a joint resolution was introduced in the Senate under the sponsorship of sixteen members. While it was never brought to a vote, it did express the thinking of many Kentucky legislators and the people they represented. It emphasized the shortage of practicing physicians in the State, the jeopardy to the health and welfare of the people from this shortage, the need that the Commonwealth should take concern over providing facilities to meet the situation, and the idea that the University of Kentucky would be a proper agency for carrying out such a program of professional education in medicine.

The growing demand for a second medical school in Kentucky came from the grassroots—from the mountains, the rural communities, the villages and small towns, the remote and out-of-the-way places. The people's voice wanted to know why they were denied medical service when there were intelligent local boys who wanted to study medicine and then to return to practice in their home communities.

While this great question was under discussion, one day four gentlemen appeared unannounced at my office to discuss the matter of medical education in Kentucky. They were physicians, one the president of the Kentucky Medical Association, one the dean of the Medical School of the University of Louisville, and two from the Council of Medical Education in the American Medical Association. Their report written after this conference stated that more adequate facilities for medical education in Kentucky were essential to the improvement of medical care in Kentucky, and that the best way of achieving this expansion was to establish a medical school in the University of Kentucky. Soon the General Assembly of 1952 directed the Legislative Research Commission to make a careful and impartial study of the desirability and steps necessary for establishing a State-supported medical school at the University of Kentucky.

Five eminent Kentucky physicians were appointed by the Governor to assist and advise the commission to study and formulate recommendations to the 1954 General Assembly. The most thorough and comprehensive study ever made of medical education in Kentucky resulted from the deliberations of the Legislative Research Commission and the Advisory Committee. In their "Long Range Plan" they recommended the formation of a "Grade A" medical school based on certain requirements:

a. The construction of a teaching hospital with a minimum capacity of 500 beds.
b. The construction of a Medical Sciences Building sufficient to accommodate classes to graduate 75 doctors per year.
c. Adequate residence halls for nurses, interns, and residents.
d. The assurance of adequate annual financial support.
e. The assurance of obtaining a competent dean and faculty.

After this report, public opinion crystallized rapidly in favor of founding a medical school at the University of Kentucky. Many candidates for the State legislature in both parties announced their support for a State-supported school of medicine. An overwhelming majority of the newspapers in the State came out in favor of the medical school. From practically all parts of the State came resolutions from luncheon clubs, from parent-teacher associations, health organizations, and farm organizations, inquiring why the University did not take the initiative and indicate its interest in the establishment of a school of medicine. Our response to such inquiries was that the University was ready to set up such a school when the

State was prepared to finance the project. To many people this response was not satisfactory. They thought that the Board of Trustees should go ahead and establish a medical college, and then request the next General Assembly to implement it by making an appropriation to finance it. At a meeting of the Board of Trustees on June 1, 1954, I took up the matter. Referring to KRS Section 164.210, I said that there was no doubt about the Board of Trustees of the University having authority to establish officially a school of medicine if, in its judgment, this was the proper time to do it. Then I said: "I am recommending that the trustees declare their interest in this project by formally establishing a College of Medicine to be opened when the General Assembly provides funds for its establishment." This recommendation was unanimously approved by the Board of Trustees, and the Medical Center came into existence on paper.

From that date until the next meeting of the General Assembly in January, 1956, a campaign in behalf of the newly created medical school was carried on by the Kentucky Medical Foundation, an organization under the leadership of certain Lexington physicians. The Kentucky Farm Bureau displayed unparalled interest in the project. Many local papers advocated its creation. Opposition to the movement came largely from Louisville and Jefferson County. Both candidates for Governor in the fall of 1955 supported the proposed medical school at the University of Kentucky. Everywhere A. B. Chandler spoke, he said emphatically that if elected, he would build the new medical school.

After Mr. Chandler's election as Governor, he notified the President of the University and the Board of Trustees that they should prepare plans for a great Medical Center, assuring them that it would be built during his administration. When the General Assembly met in January, 1956, he recommended an appropriation of $5,000,000 to begin the construction of a plant that would cost ultimately between $26,000,000 and $28,000,000, to be erected out of State and Federal funds.

Our first task after the original appropriation was made was to find an outstanding medical educator to serve as Vice President of the Medical Center and dean of the College of Medicine. We sought advice from the American Medical Association, from some of the great foundations, from the presidents of great universities that had outstanding medical schools, and from the deans of medical colleges. A list of 52 capable doctors possessing special competency in medical education was compiled. After further study, the list was reduced to ten and then to four. I invited each of these four well-known doctors to visit the University for two or three days for interviews with trustees, deans and selected professors, the Governor, outstanding physicians, and some prominent citizens. Each physician under consideration for this position met with some forty members of our committee at a luncheon, spoke on medical education, and answered questions from our group relative to his views on the subject.

After the interviews were completed, each member of the committee was given a form listing the persons under consideration and asking him to rank the persons being considered for this position. The outcome of this composite judgment showed that Dr. William R. Willard, dean of the College of Medicine of Syracuse University, was the overwhelming choice of the group. I had invited President-elect Dr. Frank Dickey to join me in the search for the Vice President of the Medical Center, and we agreed that Dr. Willard was our choice. Jointly Dr. Dickey and I recommended him to the Board of Trustees, and this recommendation was unanimously approved.

CHAPTER SIX

When a University Goes to War

*I*T is something of a coincidence that President McVey started his administration (1917) at the beginning of World War I, and that I, too, became a wartime President of the University less than six months after arriving on the campus in 1941, for in December of that year the Japanese attacked Pearl Harbor.

Immediately many of the objectives of the University were shifted from a peacetime program to preparation for war. We began to think in terms of a world at war and of the survival of our kind of civilization. The day after Pearl Harbor the deans met in my office, and we began a soul-searching deliberation on how we could help our country to meet the crisis. These meetings were continued until we had developed a program that put the University squarely into the war. Our resources in manpower, our laboratories, and our plant were all at the service of our government. Many of our professors and other staff members, some already in reserve units, went into active service; a number of the younger teachers volunteered and were immediately taken into the armed forces. Other members of the staff accepted civilian jobs in government.

The spirit with which they volunteered their services is best illustrated by the action of Dr. W. S. Webb, head of the Department of Physics, who had been a major in the artillery in World War I. He was three months past sixty when World War II broke out. Professor Webb applied to the War Department to have his commission renewed and asked for service in the artillery. He was informed that he was too old, that sixty was the age limit for service in the armed forces. Upon receipt of this information, he boarded a train for Washington, where he appealed this decision. A general and two retired colonels heard his appeal. Dr. Webb emphasized his strength and vitality, and stated that he was just as good a man as he ever was. He kept repeating that he was only three months over sixty, and that they should let him reenter active service. Finally, after he had informed the reviewing committee over and over again that he was only three months over sixty, the general who presided at the hearing interrupted him. "Sir, I want you to understand that it is not the three months that is keeping you out of the army; it is the sixty years. Case dismissed." Dr. Webb returned home somewhat abashed. However, within six months he found the Department of Physics greatly expanded. It provided instruction for more than 3,000 army trainees during the war.

Colonel Howard Donnell, professor of Military Science and Tactics, informed me upon the outbreak of war that there were 1,175 men in the ROTC unit at the University. Of this group, 983 were in the basic course and 192 in the advanced course. The training of these young men was immediately stepped up that they might be commissioned before the close of the school year. A few months after the opening of hostilities in World War II, we held a convocation honoring more than a thousand young men in the ROTC who had been called into the service of their country. Colonel B. E. Brewer, commandant of the ROTC, bade farewell to his cadets and watched practically every man in the unit leave for an army camp. Many of these boys never came home again. The young men trained on the campus of the University held every rank from second lieutenant to major general.

In 1942 the University entered into a contract with the War Department for the training of engineers. The men were sent here from the Army Engineering School at Fort Belvoir, Virginia. These men were given instruction in general drafting, topographic drafting, surveying, and geodetic computing. The army took over the Phoenix Hotel, where the men were housed. The College of Engineering gave the instruction. During a period of about one year 3,174 soldiers were enrolled. The Engineers' Specialist School closed in September, 1943. However, in May, 1943, a new organization known as the Army Specialized Training Program was initiated. During the period of its existence more than 2,000 men, representing every state in the Union as well as the District of Columbia, were enrolled as students. They occupied all our dormitories, including those for women, and the Phoenix Hotel. They were a group of very intelligent and highly selected young men. More than 5,000 men were trained in the University during the war in these two organizations, the Engineers' Specialist School and the Army Specialized Training Program.

Every college of the University took part in some form of national defense during the war years. Nearly all the younger faculty members joined the military forces. The teaching load of those instructors who did not enter military service during the war years remained heavy. They were teaching young men in uniform how to become useful in specialized fields; also, they were teaching boys not yet old enough to enter military service. In their classes were some students not physically fit for military service, and many young women pursuing college courses in preparation for civilian duties and responsibilities.

The College of Agriculture and Home Economics took the lead in increasing food production and in the preservation of food after it was produced. Dean Thomas P. Cooper's counsel was constantly sought by the agencies of the government in all problems relating to agriculture. He served on a number of important defense committees, and much of his time was spent in Washington.

The College of Engineering had heavy teaching demands made on it in the preparation of soldier-engineers. It also gave many short courses to workers in industry. Dean James H.

Graham was called to Washington by President Roosevelt, and spent about two-thirds of his time as a consultant in the War Department.

Professor E. L Gillis, long the keeper of the records of the University, agreed to make up a roll of the sons and daughters of the University of Kentucky who were in service during these tragic war years. His roster reveals that there were 7,644 men and women from the University engaged in the war, and that 334 of these died in the service. The Memorial Coliseum is a lasting monument to their memory.

CHAPTER SEVEN

Public Relations of the University

ONE of the grave responsibilities resting on the shoulders of a university president these days is the maintenance of good public relations. This is true for both public and private institutions. For an institution of learning, public relations means interpreting the service of the school to the people. Business and industry spend millions of dollars on their public-relations programs. Colleges and universities cannot ignore this function.

Many of our educational institutions today have a director of public relations and a staff of several persons working full time to create a climate of good will toward their institution both on the part of the public and on the part of its own personnel. Even though the university may have an excellent department of public relations, the president cannot escape being the chief publicity officer. He is compelled to give a considerable amount of his time to this phase of the work. There are some tasks that a president cannot delegate to others. Certain problems of public relations can be handled only by the head of the institution.

While I was President, I always tried to keep in close contact with the press and radio. I sought to be on good terms with reporters, not criticizing what they wrote, even though it was critical of our action or program. I always saw the representatives of the press and radio promptly when they called to interview me on any subject in which they had an interest.

I answered the questions they asked me, and was as frank and honest as possible, not withholding information when it was requested. This frankness resulted in my having what I regarded as a "good press" all the years I served as President. After we had prepared our biennial budget, we invited the editorial staffs of the leading newspapers in the State to have dinner with the administrative officials of the University, and at this time we presented our proposed budget. When something very unusual happened that would be regarded as news, I would call a press conference, inviting newsmen to meet at my office to share in the information I possessed. After many years of contact with newspaper and radio reporters, I can say that they have been my friends and that I have greatly enjoyed this friendship.

When I came to the University in 1941, I found an active but small Alumni Association. At that time there were only about 1,600 paid-up members. One of our public-relations problems was that of creating more interest in our graduates. This was a much harder task than I had expected. Some very loyal alumni were ready to work hard for the University, but the majority were indifferent—not antagonistic, you understand, but lukewarm, their interest being primarily in athletics rather than in a dynamic educational program.

I began my public-relations work with alumni by suggesting to those already interested in alumni activity that we form alumni clubs in a number of the larger cities of the United States where many of our former graduates lived. Already there were such clubs in New York, Chicago, and Washington. Now many other American cities have University of Kentucky alumni clubs that enjoy occasional meetings. By 1956 there were eighteen metropolitan clubs. Also, we asked that an alumni club be organized in each of the more populous counties. In sparsely populated parts of the State we urged that two, three, or even four counties join in forming a regional alumni club. Today we have 93 local alumni clubs.

I traveled to practically every county in the State, usually with the president or secretary of the Alumni Association, or some prominent alumnus, in order to get acquainted with our graduates in their after-college life. I told them many things about their Alma Mater, and outlined our program for the future. I urged them to become active representatives of the University of Kentucky, interpreting the University and its program to their local people. We asked them to visit their local high schools to tell the students about their University, and to urge those about to graduate to consider the State University when making their college plans.

In order to get out a crowd, we often took with us one of the coaches, and we would show a film of a recent football or basketball game. After the picture, one of us from the University would talk about the growth, the work, and the needs of the institution. My theme was primarily the University in the service of the State. I tried to make every person feel that he was a stockholder in the University and that it was working to help him with his problems as a citizen. I showed my audiences that we were not only educating their sons and daughters, but through our research were enriching the lives of all citizens. I talked about research that had returned millions of dollars to the farmers; about new cover crops for the farms; about improvement of seed, control of pests, better use of fertilizers, soil conservation, and other problems that farmers and homemakers constantly face. When talking with urban groups of alumni, I discussed economic problems and ways in which the University through its research was helping to improve business and industry.

In my contacts with Kentucky audiences I developed certain slogans which I repeated every time I made an address. I believed in these fundamental principles and wanted to convince my fellow citizens of their truth. Into nearly every speech I made to these alumni during my presidency I wove these two ideas in some way or other: First, you cannot have a great State without a great State University. Second, the State of Kentucky is really the campus of the University. Many thousands of people heard and believed this fundamental doctrine, and soon were helping us to build a better University and a better State.

Over a period of fifteen years our active, dues-paying alumni organized local alumni clubs with a membership of 5,266 persons. This is not enough; but with another decade, the University will have an active alumni association of 25,000 members. Then the University will find it easier to secure an adequate budget with which to serve the citizens of the State.

The officers of the Alumni Association during this decade and a half did much to arouse an interest in the association. They traveled over the State at their own expense, speaking to former graduates and to high-school students, and interpreting the University to the citizens of Kentucky. Table 4 in Appendix A gives a list of these presidents of the Alumni Association from 1941-1942 to 1956-1957. These men performed a fine service for their University in their leadership of the University's organized alumni. Praise also should be given to Miss Helen King, who, since she became executive secretary to the Alumni Association in 1946, has been an aggressive, dynamic leader in building a greater association.

As a part of our public-relations program we have been conscious of the need, as a land-grant university, to keep in close contact with the farmers of the State. In company with our field agents of the Agricultural Extension Division, I have traveled over Kentucky east and west, north and south, thousands of miles, attending all kinds of farm meetings, addressing farmers on a variety of problems of farm and home.

I lived on a farm until I was eighteen years old, and I did every kind of work that any country boy ever had to do. I really learned something about farming. Later, as the owner of a farm in Madison County, Kentucky, that produced corn, tobacco, small grain, forage crops, registered Hereford cattle, and registered sheep, I knew something about the problems of agriculture and spoke the language of farmers. I have belonged to the Farm Bureau since it was organized in Madison

County, and frequently attended their meetings and even participated on their programs. I remember particularly one farm meeting in Ohio County, Kentucky, when the program for the day consisted of visits to half a dozen farms. Dr. Wesley Garrigus was scheduled to evaluate several herds of cattle. Two farms had registered herds of Herefords, one being on the cow-and-calf plan, another farm produced feeder cattle, and two produced fat cattle. Dr. Garrigus failed to arrive. At ten o'clock the county agent announced that in the absence of Dr. Garrigus, I would analyze the cattle. I accepted the challenge; there was nothing else for me to do. Apparently I pleased the farmers. I think I never received more compliments on any effort I have ever made. Since that day the farmers of Ohio County have been wholeheartedly back of the University of Kentucky. Good public relations might have had something to do with their warm support.

In many respects the College of Agriculture and Home Economics, the Experiment Station, and the Agricultural Extension Service have the best opportunity to contact people and to live in close relations with our farmers, their wives and children. The 4-H clubs with a membership of about 75,000 boys and girls present a great opportunity to the faculty and staff of this division to know the people of the rural areas of Kentucky and for these people to know personally our professors, research personnel, field agents, and county agents. Under the leadership of both Dean Cooper and Dean Frank J. Welch a splendid public-relations program has been carried on for many years. The only criticism I have ever had of these services was that many people thought these agricultural organizations constituted the entire University.

Time and again I have gone to the Kentucky Farm Bureau asking for its support in our request for an adequate budget to support the total University. This organization has never failed me. As a result of the Farm Bureau's support, several millions of dollars came to the University. Neither did this organization fail us when political pressure was brought to bear upon the

President and the Board of Trustees to name a dean of the College of Agriculture and Home Economics that we could not recommend.

As a part of our public-relations program I joined the Lexington Chamber of Commerce. Soon I was elected to the executive committee, and I continued on this committee until I retired as President; then the Chamber made me a life member. I also worked in close harmony with the Kentucky Chamber of Commerce, attending all of their annual meetings. For seven years I was a member of the Agricultural and Industrial Development Board and took an active part in the program it fostered for bringing industry into Kentucky.

I encouraged the faculty of the College of Commerce to become allied with businessmen and business organizations, and also with leaders of labor. Dean C. C. Carpenter's work with the bankers of Kentucky did much to secure their support for a dynamic educational program. He also organized a School for Bankers which met each summer for a week on the campus. About 100 young bankers attended this school every year.

When Elvis Stahr became the dean of the College of Law in 1948, he and his professional colleagues made many contacts with the practicing lawyers of Kentucky and became active in their meetings. He brought many older lawyers to the campus for meetings of one or two days' duration, where they discussed legal problems and shared common experiences. He and other professors on his staff became acquainted with judges on the various courts and convinced these officials of the college's interest in their work. As a result of these personal and professional contacts between the law professors and the practicing lawyers in the State, the attitude of the profession toward the College of Law was much improved.

The College of Education under the administration of Dean William S. Taylor and later of its young dean, Dr. Frank Dickey, contributed greatly to the building of a better public-school system in our State. This college not only trained most of the leaders in education at the graduate level in Kentucky, but also led in the valuable educational research that has been carried on here in the past forty years. It would be difficult to improve upon the kind of public relations that the College of Education has given the University since the college was established in 1923.

The public-relations program of the University was strengthened decidedly when the College of Pharmacy became a college of the University in 1947. There are approximately 750 drugstores in Kentucky, each of these a social center where people congregate for a milkshake or a soft drink—and to hear the news. The modern drugstore has in a way taken the place of the old country store and the blacksmith shop. The pharmacist who operates a drugstore is a citizen who wields considerable influence. For 77 years Kentucky pharmacists had taken pride in their old College of Pharmacy in Louisville. When this College was integrated into the University of Kentucky, much of their interest and affection went with the College into the University. The 750 drugstores became so many centers promoting their college in the University. Thus the University of Kentucky acquired a new clientele who went to work interpreting the University and its services to our citizens. These new friends, who had confidence in Dean Slone, listened to him as he presented the needs of the University. As a result, the budget of the institution received considerable new support in areas that never before had been much interested in its problems.

The public has to be acquainted with the work of the University if the institution is to receive adequate support. Convinced of the validity of this idea, I began to work with my colleagues in 1941 with a view to getting them to support this philosophy. Most of them approved of a campaign of public relations. Gradually we employed a staff who gave all their time to the promotion of the University. This staff also worked with the professors, researchers, and all other employees to make them aware that each of them had a responsibility to promote good relations with those people with whom they were in contact. Many of the professors became conscious of this responsibility; others never caught on. What professors do, what kind of lives they live, constitute the essence of institutional relations with the public.

Those who would practice good public relations must recognize that there is no such thing as "the public." There are many publics. One must be able to recognize these publics and deal with them in relation to their various interests. The farmers represent one public, business and professional men another. Each has to have special treatment according to its particular interests and needs. Then there are the alumni, the students, the intellectuals, the sportsmen with their interest primarily fixed on winning athletic teams. No special public can be neglected if you are interested in the best public relations.

Too often there grows up between state institutions of learning and private colleges bitter rivalries, jealousies, and unwholesome competition. This kind of rivalry invariably results in envy and strife between institutions that should be working together. The history of higher education in Kentucky reveals many bitter fights between the private colleges and the University. When the A. and M. College was established in 1865, feuds between this infant institution and the six private colleges in the State immediately followed until Dr. Frank L. McVey became President of the University of Kentucky in 1917. President McVey did everything possible to allay the ill feeling that existed. At the time of his retirement in 1940, a very different atmosphere existed among these institutions.

When I became President in 1941, I resolved that I would leave no stone unturned to bring about still greater harmony and cooperation between private colleges and State colleges— and between private colleges and private colleges, State colleges and State colleges. To this end, each year I invited to Maxwell Place the college presidents and their wives in the hope that social contacts would help in solving the problem.

From time to time I visited each of the other colleges in the State, frequently speaking to their faculties and students. I never let an opportunity pass without offering praise for the contribution each college was making to the State and the nation. When the president of the Kentucky Independent College Foundation requested me to participate on a statewide radio program in behalf of the private colleges, I gladly accepted, because of my interest in their problems and activities. In this address I said: "These independent private colleges and universities are our best safeguard for the freedom of knowledge and all the freedoms guaranteed by the Bill of Rights under our Constitution. The would-be dictator knows he cannot take over our private, independent colleges or universities as he might capture a public college or university. Therefore, the private institution of higher learning is our best bulwark for perpetuation of free public colleges and universities. These private institutions must not be permitted to languish and die; they serve for the support of every citizen in Kentucky, that our intellectual freedom may be preserved."

Repeatedly I have said that Kentucky needs all her colleges, both private and public, to produce the number of college men and women which the State needs for ample leadership in the years ahead. I have thrown into the troubled waters the insistence that for a century and a half the private college has made a great contribution to higher education in Kentucky, and that it must be supported so that it can continue its good work.

CHAPTER EIGHT

Keeping the University Free

*T*HE average citizen has only a meager acquaintance with the various and sometimes vicious pressures which a college president must be able to resist. Upon his resistance, in a considerable degree, depends the survival of his college. I do not hesitate to say that one of the most serious problems I have had to face has been to keep the University free.

Many kinds of pressure are applied to educational institutions. Nearly always the pressure is applied subtly, is executed with fine art, and is ingenious. The most insidious pressures applied to state universities are those by politicians who have no interest in the university except to use it for patronage. But political pressure is not the only dominating force brought to bear upon universities. Often there is pressure from business groups, organized labor, farm organizations, religious and ecclesiastical bodies, so-called patriotic groups, and propagandists. Often the motive is to secure control of the appointment of staff members and faculty. Not infrequently the aim is to dictate the content of the curriculum, with insistence that certain subjects be taught. Sometimes the intent is to serve as censors of the professors in the fields of economics, sociology, political science, history, and religion.

An important function of the college president is to stand guard over his institution against these numerous pressure groups and provide the teacher and researcher with a climate conducive to objective teaching and the search for truth. No matter how heavy is the pressure on the president, he must stand like Horatio at the bridge and let no one pass to destroy the freedom of the classroom and laboratory.

Pressure on the administration and faculty is frequently exerted through a process of intimidation, a threat to do something unless the president or professor complies with the views of the party making the threat, an old trick well known to college administrators. The paper from which the following paragraphs are taken is an example of such pressure. It was written by a man who had entered the primary election in 1947 with the hope of securing the nomination for Governor. In the smoothest of language he called attention to a recent article in the University Extension Bulletin on the urgent need for amending the 1890 Constitution of the Commonwealth of Kentucky. In this letter he closed with these words:

> All citizens, including those who edit the University Extension Bulletin, have a right to express their views on the question of calling a Constitutional Convention, but none of us have the right to propagandize our ideas on controversial political issues at the taxpayers' expense.
>
> Knowing you as I do, I am sure that you will agree with me as to the proprieties in this matter, and I am confident that you will take whatever steps are necessary to prevent the facilities of the University from being used in an unfair and unlawful manner.

How should a college president react to this kind of challenge? I replied in part:

> So long as I am President of the University of Kentucky, I am going to protect the professors of this institution in their right of freedom of speech and academic freedom as generally recognized. I do not want our professors at the University to belong to the neuter gender. If they are so negative in character as not to feel the desire to express their opinions about great social and moral issues, they would not be worth the salt that goes into their bread.
>
> ... I personally was one of the early advocates of a new Constitution. I discussed this subject at a convocation under the direction of the Student Government Association on October 12, 1945. This

address was published, and my views on the subject are well known to the people of the State.

In reply, the gentleman threatened to take legal action if the University continued what he called "advocacy of a new State constitution in its publications." This threat we ignored, and we heard nothing more of the matter.

Most public colleges and universities have at some time or other been subjected to political pressures that have handicapped them in their development. This almost happened to the University of Kentucky when the General Assembly of 1950 amended the statutes by directing the Division of Personnel in the Department of Finance to "prepare a schedule of compensation, payable out of the State Treasury, with minimum and maximum salary rates . . . for the office or position of employment in every constitutional administrative department. . . . Such schedules shall be based upon studies of the duties and responsibilities of the offices. . . . No such schedule shall become effective until it has been approved by the Governor."

Since the State institutions of higher learning were included within the Department of Education, this legislation would have placed every employee of the University and of the State colleges under the Department of Personnel and the Governor. This legislation was designed to take from the Board of Trustees of the University and the boards of regents of the State colleges their power to define positions and to fix salaries. The bill had passed the House before I was aware of its introduction. In the Senate I protested, but without success. Immediately after this bill became law, I informed the Southern Association of Colleges and Secondary Schools, the American Association of Colleges of Teacher Education, and other accrediting agencies in regard to this action of the General Assembly. These organizations promptly went into action.

From the Southern Association I received a letter stating that such legislation was a violation of the declaration of principles of the Southern Association and in conflict with its constitution and standards, and jeopardized the membership of the University and the State colleges in the Southern Association. The American Association of Colleges for Teacher Education viewed with grave concern the existence of "statutory provisions which deprive Boards of Trustees . . . of their control of educational institutions . . . by taking from them the power to administer the affairs of these institutions." They gave warning that any such law was likely to interfere with their retention on the accredited list. I notified the Board of Trustees, the University Faculty, and the local chapter of the American Association of University Professors of the humiliation that was likely to come upon higher public education in Kentucky from such legislation.

A committee of the American Association of University Professors prepared a scholarly brochure entitled "Relationship between the State Government and the University of Kentucky: Report and Recommendations, March, 1951." It analyzed the issues logically, concisely, and courageously. Allan M. Trout called it a "declaration of independence," saying that it was one of the boldest steps ever taken in public higher education in Kentucky. The press of the State placed the issue squarely before the people. Professors, deans, and the President made many addresses on this subject to the people of the State. Soon there was a climate of opinion throughout Kentucky demanding that this law be repealed. Candidates for public office in both parties began to advocate the repeal of this legislation. When the General Assembly met in 1952, it unanimously amended the law so as to restore to the controlling boards the right to appoint employees and fix salaries in the State University and State colleges.

I feel sure that this victory saved these institutions from being dropped by the accrediting agencies of the country, and also saved them from a humiliation that would have been difficult to overcome.

One of the most difficult problems relative to keeping the

KEEPING THE UNIVERSITY FREE

University free was what has been known as the Wenner-Gren Laboratory controversy. This aeronautical laboratory about which so much trouble was raised was built before I came to the University as its President. The project was initiated under my predecessor, Dr. McVey, and was built when Dr. Thomas P. Cooper was Acting President, 1940-1941. Colonel James H. Graham, dean of the College of Engineering in the University, had made contact with Alex L. Wenner-Gren, a Swedish industrialist and founder of the Viking Foundation, in July, 1940, and had secured a gift from him for an aeronautical research laboratory costing $97,000 for construction and $53,000 for equipment.

Shortly after the beginning of World War II, Mr. Wenner-Gren was placed on the block list by the State Department. Then gossip and rumors were spread by a small group of men seeking personal revenge against Colonel Graham, and also against Judge Richard C. Stoll, a faithful member of the Board of Trustees for more than fifty years. All kinds of fantastic tales were spread: There were spies and traitors connected with the laboratory. There must be secret communication with the Nazis by radio. The propaganda produced hysteria in some people. I had a careful investigation made by the FBI and by intelligence agents of the War Department. I was informed that the Federal government was satisfied about the laboratory. The War Department and the Pratt-Whitney Aircraft Corporation continued to use the laboratory during the war. The army had soldiers taking courses there during practically the entire war.

Early in 1944 two Fayette County men and their attorney called at my office one afternoon and inisisted upon seeing me. At the time, I was presiding at a faculty meeting, but they informed my secretary that their business was so important that they would wait. When the faculty meeting adjourned, I gave them an interview. They informed me that they held me in high esteem personally, that they thought I was making a good President, and that they wanted to help me. They attacked Dean Graham and Judge Stoll, charging that these men were running the University for their own aggrandizement. They felt sorry for me because I was under the control of two such domineering persons. They charged Dean Graham with drawing a salary that he did not earn, since he spent his time in Washington and was not giving any service to the University. They said that other trustees were under the domination of Judge Stoll, and that the Board of Trustees had broken the law by paying Dean Graham's salary while he was in Washington. They told me that they were going to bring suit against Dean Graham, Comptroller Peterson, and the trustees. All they wanted me to do was to remain quiet, to take no stand one way or the other, and I would not be hurt. However, if I attempted to defend any of these, they would include me in the suit.

"Is this blackmail?" I asked when they had finished. Then the men became offensive in their attitude toward me. Reminding them that it was my dinnertime and that I was having guests, I asked them to excuse me from further discussion. The meeting adjourned in a tense atmosphere.

In March, 1944, the suit was filed in the Franklin Circuit Court against Dean Graham, Comptroller Peterson, and certain trustees. After many witnesses had been heard, Colonel Graham was called to the witness stand. He told of his connection with the University and of the request from President Roosevelt in 1941 that he serve as a consultant to the War Department. He said that he had received $1.00 per year for 23 months. Then the undersecretary of war had placed him on a salary of $8,000 a year, beginning March 16, 1943, because the Federal government no longer employed dollar-a-year men. He told about the approximate amounts of time he gave the University and the War Department. He answered questions bearing on the Wenner-Gren Laboratory until the presiding judge overruled further questions on that subject.

Later, when Judge Ardery addressed the jury, he said, "No testimony has been introduced upon which I can submit this case to you for your free consideration. The testimony showed that Colonel Graham rendered substantial services for the salary paid him out of the funds of the University of Kentucky. There was no evidence introduced that he was paid without rendering commensurate services. It is now my duty to find for each and every one of the defendants, and it is my duty so to direct you."

The following editorial appeared in the Lexington *Herald-Leader* on May 12, 1946, summarizing the long-drawn-out fight designed to injure the University and discredit some of us who were connected with the institution:

The whole state should be glad to have these disputes disposed of, the name of the University cleared, and its work and prestige strengthened. The legislature showed its confidence in the institution and its management by doubling the largest appropriation ever made in the past. So the agitation passes like a summer day.

A petition signed by seventeen students asked for a public hearing on the gift to the University of the Aeronautical Research Laboratory. Governor Willis requested from the University a complete and documented report from the time of the initial negotiations for the laboratory until the date of the filing of the petition. He requested Vice President Chamberlain to prepare this material. His report was one of the most complete official documents I have ever examined, a brochure entitled: "The Facts. A Report on the Aeronautical Research Laboratory, University of Kentucky, 1945." This report closed the controversy. The laboratory today is one of the great assets of the University.

In the following year an investigating committee appointed by the Kentucky House of Representatives made a long report expressing their complete satisfaction in the conduct of the President and trustees of the University in the controversy, praising their dignified and tolerant attitude toward their attackers, and suggesting that students or faculty members who continued in their dissatisfaction toward the administration would do well to "promply disassociate themselves therefrom and seek the benefit of higher education elsewhere."

The next instance of pressure of which I shall speak was contained in a request made by a Protestant church. It was made by men of good will, always polite and gracious. They believed in their request, and persisted in pushing it to the limit. We felt that it must be denied.

In 1948 certain officers of the General Association of Baptists in Kentucky, heading a committee of very able ministers, requested that the University of Kentucky establish a cooperative program involving Bible courses. They insisted that their plan had been implemented in some other state Universities, and could see no reason why the University of Kentucky should not likewise accept it. Having always held that our "founding fathers" were wise in insisting on the separation of the church and the state, I raised a number of objections to the proposed plan. They answered my objections to their own satisfaction, but I did not acquiesce in their views. Then I requested the committee to give me a written statement of their request, stating that I would give it due consideration and secure the views of others.

In their lengthy reply they said that they wished the University to permit them to give these courses in religion as electives, open to all students, each course carrying three hours credit. They said that their plan safeguarded the separation of church and state, and that it was a method of providing religious instruction for students who desired to study the Bible. The courses which they would like to offer would include a survey of the Old Testament, a survey of the New Testament, a study of the life and teachings of Jesus, and a course in the Acts and the Epistles with emphasis on the spread of Christianity.

I asked the office of the attorney general of Kentucky to advise me as to whether the University of Kentucky could legally offer such a program. The question was referred to Assistant Attorney General M. B. Holifield, a very able constitutional lawyer. After a long and thorough study of the case, he gave an opinion against the teaching of such courses in the State University. His argument was that the University of Kentucky, being an arm of the State government, could not perform any activity prohibited by the State Constitution. This would mean a tax-supported institution was giving aid to a church, sectarian, or denominational school in contravention to Section 189. For a tax-supported school to place its imprimatur upon a course of study emphasizing the Divine Message as set forth in the Bible would certainly be giving aid in religious work in contravention to the prohibitions of the First and Fourteenth Amendments to the Federal Constitution as construed by the Supreme Court of the United States. He added the personal note that he himself was a Missionary Baptist, and this legal opinion represented not his religious convictions, but the views of State and Federal Constitutions as construed by the courts of last resort in these sovereignties.

While this opinion was not entirely satisfactory to the Baptist committee, they soon dropped the matter. It is only fair to say that the University did everything it could legally do to develop a program of moral and spiritual education, and this program attracted national interest. The University urged its students to identify themselves with the churches of their choice while they were in college. Full cooperation was given student pastors supported by local churches. We left the teaching of religion up to the local churches, but the University encouraged students to participate in church activities in their preferred churches.

Some pressures come from within the University. Deans and heads of departments will insist that their college or department is in great need of expansion. A dean will insist that another department must be established in his college, or it will lose what prestige it already has. Sometimes he will get alumni to bring pressure on the President with the hope of achieving his end. A department head will frequently insist that another professor must be added to his staff, and that new courses will have to be offered to maintain the standard of the department. At the same time this expansion is being urged, there is a general and very strong demand for increase of salaries. It is my conviction that professors have done much to keep their salaries down by continually demanding additional staff members to expand the offerings of their departments. Salary increases that they might have received go to pay new instructors to teach new courses, often added without real justification.

Traditionally the curriculum of a university is controlled by the faculty, not by the trustees or the administrative officers of the institution. When a department requests faculty permission to add another series of courses, faculty courtesy demands that other departments acquiesce. This policy is somewhat analogous to senatorial courtesy in legislative bodies. By this method, departments add one course after another, and the catalog grows thicker by the year. As University President I witnessed this proliferation with alarm, but I was helpless to stem the tide. This type of pressure from the faculty makes costs of instruction mount and keeps faculty salaries low. In no area of higher education is there greater need for reform. Under present and accepted modes of operation this reform can only be brought about by the faculty.

During the years I have served as a college president, I have known pressures from every segment of society, from politicians, businessmen, labor leaders, farmers, preachers, physicians, professors, and students. My policy has been to receive every petitioner courteously, listen attentively to his story, consider his request with deliberation, analyze the logic and reasonableness of his petition, and reach the conclusion that appeared to be in the best interests of the institution over which I presided. I refused to be swayed by pressure alone, no matter how persistent it might be. A man who cannot withstand pressure has no business being a college president. To yield to all the demands that are made upon him in a single year would wreck his institution.

CHAPTER NINE

The Vanishing University Trustee

SINCE the establishment of the earliest colleges in America, both public and private, charters and statutory provisions have provided for boards of trustees or regents to determine and administer policies for these institutions of higher learning. In order to provide for the greatest amount of freedom in teaching, our founding fathers saw the necessity for independent governing bodies for institutions that were created to give instruction to the youth of our country. On the whole, the charters, body of laws, and, in a number of instances, state constitutions have given these governing boards very broad authority and have not encumbered their work by limiting their control over the colleges and universities.

Through statutory provisions Kentucky, like other states in the Union, early placed its institutions of higher education in the hands of boards of trustees or regents, and made it possible for these boards to act on their own best judgment with regard to the administration of these institutions. Only in recent years has there been a tendency to take away from governing boards their administrative authority, and to transfer to other State agencies one power after another. State agencies are chipping away the authority long exercised by the trustees of educational institutions, and the universities are slipping away from them. The issue is whether the trustees and the president administer the university, or someone else runs the university. Rapidly we are nearing the time when very little authority will reside in a board of trustees or regents, except by sufferance of those agencies that actually have control over many of the college activities. While the powers and duties of the trustees and regents are being eroded from time to time, the public is scarcely aware of what is taking place.

Trustees are generally appointed by the governor, but in a few states they are elected by the people. The length of their term is usually longer than that of other state officials, four years being about the minimum term found in any state, and terms of six, eight, ten, and even twelve years being not uncommon. Governors usually reappoint trustees when their terms expire. The office is not commonly regarded as political. A strong public sentiment has developed in this country that the trustee of a college or university should be free of any political entanglements, so that he should be completely independent in his deliberations as a member of its governing board. Boards of college trustees have been on the whole the most independent bodies to be found in our society. The subtle attack on their authority has been so stealthy that many trustees are not yet aware of what had happened to these boards. Unless this trend is reversed, the trustee will shortly discover that he is a figurehead with little control over the institution that he is supposed to guide and direct.

The "Executive Budget," promoted with great enthusiasm by the Council of State Governments, has done much to transfer the control of all state expenditures, including that of the public-supported institutions of higher education, from the boards or officials of these agencies to the chief executive. The legislative authority for the executive budget may be in conflict with laws that long ago gave the boards of control the authority to manage their own financial affairs. Often without formally repealing these long-established laws, budgetary administrative officers and agencies have moved in and taken complete control over all financial affairs of the state educational institutions.

Richard H. Plock, secretary of the Association of Governing Boards of State Universities and Allied Institutions, said in 1957:

> These officers and agencies (State Comptrollers, State Personnel Directors, State Budget Directors, State Purchasing Agents, Pre-Auditors, State Building Authorities, State Boards of Public Works, and the like) have found the task so complicated that they have invariably had to delegate their authority to subordinates and clerks in their departments. Expenditures for public education have been subjected to the same rules as apply to expenditures for all departments of state government. Who, then, can be said to control education in such states? Is it the governing board having legal responsibility for doing so? Is it the administrative officers of the institution? Or is it actually a subordinate in a political department of the state government?

As a matter of fact, today in many states practical control of state universities is no longer under the direction of the president and his board of trustees, but is exercised by subordinates—second, third, or fourth assistant controllers, purchasing agents, budget directors—bright young men with little experience, but with abundance of confidence in their ability to direct the affairs of a complex institution of higher education.

Where is all this leading? Will it eventually lead to political control of state universities and state colleges by officers at the state capital, leaving presidents and trustees only ceremonial functions on public occasions? This is the way it is done in many countries of Europe. Are we willing to revert to that type of control for our public colleges and universities? It is an old adage that he who holds the purse string holds control within his hands. Probably most of our governors do not desire to control our educational institutions. Why should they? They are usually responsible for appointing members of the board of trustees. Can't they trust their own appointees with the management of the institutions?

In recent years a false doctrine has been spread that a state college or university is just another agency of the state and that its administration should be handled in the same manner as any other state agency. This is apparently the philosophy of the Council of State Governments. Those who propose such a false propaganda line are ignorant of the history and philosophy of higher education in the United States. Universities have never been "just another agency." From their origin in this country they have been different from political agencies of the state. They have been unique, designedly different from other agencies of the state. They are original, indigenous institutions, a product of American genius, made to fit the needs of a new kind of government. They represent the American way in education, providing for free institutions under the supervision of free men, who in turn understand that the only way to keep these institutions free is to have them divorced from political practices. Boards of control started with Harvard, and they have continued down to the present in public and private institutions of learning. Shall we in the United States overthrow more than three centuries of experience in controlling higher education by the device of boards of trustees or regents, and turn the management over to third- and fourth-class assistants and clerks in a political department?

We are not challenging the integrity of these minor officials, but we do have grave apprehension as to their ability, experience, and wisdom in the administration of so complicated an organization as a state university.

Moreover, we are fearful of what will happen to these free institutions in time if they fall completely under the control of political departments that change their personnel with every upset in the hurly-burly of politics. The bureaucrats will not be satisfied with handling the finances of the universities; they will eventually reach out and take control over the personnel of these institutions. Elsewhere there already have been cases of interference in such vital matters as personnel management, the purchase of specialized supplies and equipment, publications, professional affiliations, and in the location and planning of buildings.

When I became President of the University of Kentucky, the

University and the State colleges each prepared a budget which it presented to the Governor and the General Assembly. Representatives of each institution were invited to appear before the joint appropriations committee of the General Assembly and present their justifications for the requests. When the budget was passed, the University and each State college received a lump sum appropriated for the support of that institution for the biennium, including capital appropriations. The trustees and regents administered this budget, and through them, and them alone, each institution erected its own buildings, insured its buildings against fire and other hazards, purchased its own equipment, prepared its salary schedules within the limits of the statutory laws and the Constitution, appointed its professors and other staff members, and determined all matters of policy related to the institution.

By contrast, today the trustees or regents cannot present a budget directly to the Governor or to the legislature. It must submit its budget to the Department of Finance, where its requests may be changed or modified by those who frequently have little concept of the needs of the University. It cannot purchase a piece of equipment or a book for the library or food for its dining halls. It cannot enter into a contract; it has no voice in determining the amount of insurance to carry on its buildings; it cannot employ an architect and plan its buildings, or do many of the things which were its exclusive province. The boards cannot present directly to the General Assembly their needs for capital funds for the erection of buildings or the purchase of equipment. Neither are they permitted even to decide what buildings or what equipment is to be purchased.

Each effort to limit the independence of these boards is inevitably a move in the direction of controlling institutional policies and programs. If a state does not delegate to boards of trustees the management of these public institutions within certain broad limits of power set out in the charter or in legislation, then it has no reason to justify the establishment of boards of trustees.

The people of this country have very wisely recognized that the best protection for an institution of higher learning is to place it under the control of a board of liberal-minded, public-spirited, well-qualified citizens, and permit them to operate free of any political control. If there is an infringement of this principle, sooner or later there will come into power an administration that will take away from the professor his freedom to teach the truth as he sees it and to carry on independent research. This control can be very subtly exercised when the professor's salary may be fixed by a director of personnel who has no responsibility for, or connection with, a public college or university, and who may also be a political appointee.

I therefore earnestly appeal to the trustees everywhere, and to the people at large, to exercise their influence to halt this creeping paralysis that will sooner or later destroy the freedom of our institutions of higher education.

CHAPTER TEN

Student Citizenship on the Campus

As I mentioned in a previous chapter, President Patterson enrolled every student and was each student's adviser. I have often coveted this privilege and wished I could have such intimate contact with students. It is from these associations with students that the most satisfactory rewards come to an educator. In a large institution enrolling several thousand students, the contacts with students must, of course, be limited; but the door to the president's office should never be entirely closed.

The president has a great responsibility to communicate to the students as well as to the faculty what is going on in the university. The minutes of the board of trustees and of the faculty should be accessible to the students. A house organ that reports the activities of the campus can be used to good advantage to keep the citizens of the campus informed. It is well for the president to speak to the staff and to the students about the program of the university; the better informed they are, the happier they will be. Uninformed people often start rumors, and most of these are false. Keep the lines of communication always open between the administration, the faculty, and the students, if you expect to have good morale in the institution.

There are many kinds of student pressures brought to bear upon college administrators. These usually are not serious, but they can be very annoying. An example of this kind of thing is the demand often made by students for a holiday after the football team has won a game over a traditional rival. I have sometimes commented that college students are about the only people in the country who will pay for a product—that is to say, education—and then refuse to take it home with them. To get out of school for a day or to have the Christmas vacation extended for a few days gives most students great joy. The college president who refuses to yield to these pressures is often regarded as a killjoy and a grumpy old tyrant. He must stand fast, however, and insist that the calendar is to be followed as published.

The personnel of a college staff makes up what I choose to call the presidency, and includes among others some counselors who advise students as to their living arrangements, work, social life, and conduct as citizens of the campus and community. In this University they are called dean of men, dean of women, and dean of students. These officials perform a very useful service for young college students, especially for those living away from home for the first time. Actually they are *in loco parentis,* always ready to give counsel to students in need of guidance.

During the years when I was President of the University, three different deans of men and one dean of women served with me, Dr. T. T. Jones, Dr. A. D. Kirwan, Dr. Leslie Martin, and Mrs. Sarah Bennett Holmes. Each of these persons rendered yeoman service in guiding young students.

Dean Jones was especially helpful in assisting students who were in financial difficulties during the depression years. He secured jobs for many young men and women who would have had to drop out of school without this aid. He skillfully managed the University's Student Loan Fund so as to keep students in college. At the same time he insisted that every loan must eventually be repaid. Scarcely a dollar of this fund was lost, although a few out-of-state borrowers attempted to repudiate their obligation. He made each debtor discharge his obligation when he began to earn an income. The fact that the University has a Student Loan Fund today of more than $100,000 is largely due to the good management of Dean Jones, and later to the administration of the fund by Dean C. C. Carpenter, who took charge of it after Dean Jones retired.

About two years before Dean Jones reached the age of retirement under the governing regulations of the University, Coach A. D. Kirwan came to my office (1945) soon after the football season and said that he wished to resign as football coach. He stated emphatically that he would never coach another football team and that we should begin looking for a coach for the next year. When convinced that he meant what he said, I asked him what he intended to do. He told me that he loved to teach, and that he planned to enter Duke University to complete his work for a doctorate in history. I proposed to him that if he would enter Duke and secure his Ph.D. degree in history, which would take him about two years, I would recommend him as an associate professor of history and dean of men, since Dr. Jones would be retiring when Coach Kirwan had completed his work. I further stated that I would provide for him half salary on a leave of absence, as was made possible by the governing regulations of the Board, and would help him to secure a scholarship. He accepted the offer, went to Duke University, and made an outstanding record. Although the Duke officials made him an offer to stay with them, he declined their invitation and returned to the University of Kentucky in 1947.

World War II had just closed, and thousands of veterans were returning to the University to continue their education. A multitude of problems resulted from the return of former soldiers, sailors, and marines to the campus. There was a great shortage of housing; not enough classrooms were available to accommodate the students; and there was a serious shortage of teachers. These factors resulted in considerable unrest among the battle-worn veterans, some of whom thought that now that they had won the war, they should have preferred treatment. They organized a veterans' club with a view to dominating the administration of the University. This they might have done, if the dean of men had not been a tower of strength, a man with knowledge and skill in dealing with young men.

A small number among the more than five thousand veterans in the University had formed bad habits as a result of years of living under primitive conditions. Their delinquencies could not be tolerated on a University campus. Consequently Dean Kirwan had a number of disciplinary problems. These he handled with rare wisdom. The veterans soon saw that a high standard of personal conduct prevailed in the University community and that laxity of behavior would not be tolerated. They accepted the leadership of the dean of men, and helped him in establishing a high standard of citizenship in Cooperstown, Shawneetown, and in the dormitories, a standard that has seldom been equaled in this country. Each village was presided over by its own mayor and council. No town or village in Kentucky under 10,000 population probably had as much talent as was to be found in each of these veteran villages. These young people were a highly selected group and possessed unusual intelligence. They represented Kentucky's future leaders, and they will hold prominent positions in our society during the next fifty years.

The office of dean of women of the University of Kentucky has been filled by a number of remarkable women who have made a fine contribution to American education and who have made the position of dean of women more highly respected in this country. The roll of this distinguished group includes, among others, the names of Frances Jewell (Mrs. Frank L. McVey), Sarah Blanding, and Mrs. Sarah Bennett Holmes.

Soon after I became President in 1941 I recommended Mrs. Sarah B. Holmes to the trustees for appointment as dean of women. She remained in this position during my entire administration. The University never had a more intelligent and conscientious worker in its service than Mrs. Holmes. She was the mother of two sons and two daughters. The early death of her husband, Dr. Holmes, had made it necessary for her to support and educate these children. They are enough to prove that she knew how to guide youth from adolescence to maturity and to direct young lives into successful careers. What she did for her own children she has also done for literally thousands of young women (and some young men) who have been students of the University. She has been an intelligent administrator upon whose wisdom I have often drawn in planning the program of the University.

Many of the problems of the dean of men and the dean of women are similar, and these two officials need to work together to find the answers. The so-called "panty raids" which swept the country from New England to California are among the examples that could be cited to show the necessity of close cooperation. When this craze reached Kentucky in its moving across the land like a plague, a very serious riot occurred. Dean Holmes and Dean Kirwan were immediately alerted, and both were soon in the midst of the rioters, Mrs. Holmes in Jewell Hall to protect that citadel, Dean Kirwan on the outside attempting to quell the rioters. One young intruder who was mounting the stairs met the dean of women armed with a wet floormop, which she wrapped around his head with a flourish. This, it was said, was the only raider who penetrated the barriers of Jewell Hall.

The "panty raid" was no tea party. It continued far into the night as the marauders moved from dormitory to dormitory, from one sorority house to another. Deans, house mothers, campus police, and others readily identified the ringleaders. Later, the affair was investigated by the Vice President of the University, the dean of men, the dean of women, and the Judicial Committee of the Student Government Association. They called in the leaders of the mob, gave them an opportunity to defend themselves, and finally decided that the chief ringleaders should be suspended from the University for a stated period of time.

It is the rule that the verdict of the Judiciary Committee of the Student Government Association shall be reported first to the dean of men or to the dean of women. If suspension or expulsion is recommended, the sentence must be approved by the President before it becomes final. I approved the verdict of the Judiciary Committee of the Student Government Association and upheld the dean of men in his action. As a matter of fact, I never reversed the judgment of the dean of men or the dean of women while I was President.

In this case there were several young men who came from prominent and influential families. Some of the parents brought considerable pressure to bear upon me to reverse the finding of the student committee. On behalf of one young man I received letters, telephone calls, and personal interviews from two former Governors, two United States senators, a well-known judge, newspaper editors, and various other people. I stood my ground in spite of the fact that this boy's father was one of my very good friends, a man whom I admired and trusted. I still believe, however, that I was right in my stand. I think this boy is a better man today than he would have been if I had yielded to the entreaties of his friends.

After Dean Kirwan had served successfully for years in his position as dean of men, he came to me requesting that he be relieved of administrative duties in order that he might give all his time to teaching and research in history. Reluctantly I granted his request. As his successor we appointed Dr. Leslie L. Martin, a young psychologist who had majored in the field of personnel work. Since taking over the position of dean of men, he has done a remarkable job in working with thousands of young men students.

The major enemy of scholarship today is the automobile. Those parents who send their sons and daughters to college with a car are making it hard for their children to earn a respectable scholarship record. Students with automobiles spend too many of their weekends on the highways instead of in the laboratories and the library "digging in" on their studies.

Furthermore, the automobile offers a constant temptation to a youth to break traffic regulations, especially when he mixes gasoline with alcohol. There are other temptations, too, that are even more serious, when a car is at the disposal of an immature college youth. As a consequence of all this joyriding, students frequently break the law and are arrested by the police. Dean Martin has been exceptionally effective in working with the police and with local courts to adjudicate such cases, as well as other law infractions with which students are charged. Often these young offenders are put on probation and placed under supervision of the dean of men. Such a sentence usually works out satisfactorily and saves the boy and his family from the disgrace of a fine or a jail sentence.

About a year after Dr. Martin assumed his duties as dean of men, he encountered the most serious disciplinary problem that I have known in any college or university. The wise and courageous manner in which he handled this problem marks him as an excellent administrator, just the kind of person who should supervise the conduct of young men enrolled in the University.

In the fall of 1955 a group of hoodlums, all freshmen, enrolled in the University. The apparent leader was a lad of superior intelligence who had won a $500 scholarship because of his high standing on both achievement and intelligence tests, and had an excellent high-school record. Ten or twelve like-minded young men evidently formed an association of junior gangsters. During the fall and early winter these students were engaged regularly in criminal activities such as breaking into coin-operated machines (more than thirty such incidents occurred on the campus), wiring pinball machines in stores and taverns in order to collect money for games, and entering and robbing business houses. Two or three of the suspects were engaged in an even more dangerous activity, that of buying, transporting, and using narcotics.

During this period explosions occurred in Bradley Hall and Kinkead Hall, dormitories for men, and in Frazee Hall, a classroom building. The last of these explosions resulted in a fire that caused damage estimated at $130,000. These blasts were caused by some type of simulated bomb. The dean of men, the city police, and the fire marshal made a thorough investigation of these incidents, but the students' misplaced loyalty made it impossible to gather sufficient evidence to indict any individual. However, the names of three of the gang came out repeatedly in later interviews, indicating that they might have been implicated in the crimes.

In January, 1956, I requested Dean Martin to take the narcotics matter to the Federal narcotics agent and the city police. The representative of the Federal Narcotics Bureau agreed to provide an undercover agent who would be entered in the University as a student at the opening of the second semester, February 8. A very intelligent young man enrolled and was assigned a room in the dormitory where the junior gangsters lived. Shortly after he entered the dormitory, he was rooming with the leader of the gang. Twenty days later, March 1, at 5:30 a.m., the city police surrounded the dormitory and arrested all the students suspected of participation in the criminal acts. The plans for these operations were so carefully worked out and executed that no students other than those involved were disturbed by the police officers. Altogether twelve individuals, including ten students and two outsiders whom the suspects had brought into the dormitory to help them in their criminal activities, were taken to the police department and lodged in jail.

It seems almost incredible that a group of junior gangsters should enter the University and declare that an education would make them more efficient in their crime and help them in evading the law. They told the undercover agent that they had deliberately selected the University campus for their business because no one expects to find criminals and serious crime among college students.

On March 2, 1956, the day after the arrest of these young gangsters, the Lexington *Leader* published this editorial:

University of Kentucky officials acted commendably and unselfishly in the investigation which led to the breaking up of a gang of student hoodlums on the campus. Although President H. L. Donovan, Dean of Men Leslie L. Martin and others realized full well that the eventual publicity would not be pleasant for the University, they made no attempt to conceal the fact that the gang was at work, but instead called in law-enforcement officers and cooperated fully in the investigation.

. . . The probe has brought out that the gang . . . had organized some time ago and had selected the University of Kentucky as a sort of "sanctuary," believing they could carry on their illicit operations here without molestation. University officials, they thought, would not expose them for fear of resulting bad publicity. They also planned to gain sufficient education to enable them, later when they became big-time gangsters, to avoid arrest. . . . The abrupt termination of their ambitions certainly will serve as a warning to any other young people, here or in other universities, who might be tempted to engage in criminal activities.

Through this whole unsavory ordeal Dean Martin displayed great acumen, keen discernment, and longsuffering patience. He seems to have made no mistakes in the manner in which he handled this extraordinary problem of young gangsters on the campus.

This trying situation led me to do harder thinking than I had ever done before on the subject of discipine on a college campus. I find myself in agreement with Dr. William Oxley Thompson, the experienced president of Ohio State University, on the question of college discipline. In a paper given in 1905 to the Land Grant Association in Washington on "Discipline— Student Control," he said:

Colleges are steadily going out of the nursery business. . . . In State institutions the force and power of the State is behind college administration. This fact should be clearly and persistently set forth. . . . College authorities should turn over to the state authorities every offender. It may appear rigid and cold in the first instance or two, but there will be a long interval between troubles. In my own experience I have not hesitated to declare that the law of the state should be enforced and that I should regard any destruction of property or interference with the rights of citizens or students as proof of a kind of citizenship that could not be endured in a college. I believe that American students respect an administration that respects itself and respects the law of the land. In a college, as elsewhere, the cure for disorder is a high order of citizenship. Let the high ideals of a genuine democracy inspire the college and we shall have less of hazing, of dishonorable college traditions, but more of scholarship, of college fellowship, and social service.

When students are old enough to enter college and intelligent enough to meet the requirements of college entrance, they certainly are sufficiently mature to understand what constitutes good citizenship. They should not be regarded as juveniles, but as intelligent young adults who know how to conduct themselves. If they are old enough to drive an automobile, they are old enough to accept the responsibilities of a driver of a car. Recently we amended the Constitution of Kentucky so as to give young people the right to vote when they are eighteen years of age. If they are old enough to exercise the rights of citizenship, they are mature enough to obey the laws of the state. When they defy and break the laws of the state, they should be held responsible before the courts. They must recognize the supremacy of the law. The question of college discipline is largely solved when students recognize that the administration of the institution, in the spirit of justice, will enforce the laws of the college and the state fairly and squarely, and that there will be no disposition to cover things up and let them go free.

It has been my unhappy duty over a long period of years to suspend a number of students for a short period of time and to expel a few students permanently. Some of those whom I have had to discipline severely have come to me later, often some years later, and thanked me for taking this action. Some of them have said that it was the best thing that had ever happened to them. Sometimes it took a shock like this to bring a man to himself.

CHAPTER ELEVEN

Integration at the University

In 1948 a young Negro named John Wesley Hatch applied for admission to the College of Law. Until that time we had never received an application from a Negro for admission to the University. We recognized immediately that we faced a delicate problem which must be handled with care and wisdom. We presented the request for admission of this Negro applicant to the trustees for their advice, and were directed to obtain an opinion from the attorney general.

This official advised us that the so-called Day Law made the teaching of Negroes and white students in the same school an offense. He further stated that this law, enacted by the General Assembly in 1904, had been declared constitutional by the Supreme Court in 1908 in the Berea College case, and that it was still in full force and effect. The Day Law provided for a fine of $1,000 for any person or corporation that violated it, and an additional fine of $100 for each day the violation continued after the conviction. Neither the administrative officials nor the law professors who were counseling us relished the idea of being taken into court to test the validity of the Day Law at that time. The attorney general informed us that if we admitted a Negro into the University, he would be compelled to ask the court to uphold the validity of the Day Law.

Finally the Board of Trustees recommended that we request the Kentucky State College at Frankfort to admit the applicant with the understanding that the University would provide the teachers to instruct this Negro law student. Two able lawyers were employed part time to give this young man instruction, and arrangements were made for his use of the law library in the Capitol. After one semester the student withdrew from our improvised law school, and thus ended the project that had been designed as a solution to the problem.

Later a new approach was made by the NAACP to open the doors of the University to Negroes. A suit was filed by Lyman T. Johnson, a graduate of Virginia Union University (A.B.), and the University of Michigan (M.A.), for admission to the Graduate School of the University of Kentucky, for the purpose of pursuing graduate study in history leading to a Ph.D. degree. Mr. Johnson met all the educational requirements for admission. The Day Law alone barred his entrance.

The suit was brought in the Federal District Court before Judge H. Church Ford at Lexington. A number of distinguished Negro lawyers represented Johnson. Assistant Attorney General Holifield presented the case for the defendants. In spite of the fact that the United States Supreme Court had upheld the Day Law in 1908, we were reasonably certain that the District Court would direct us to admit Mr. Johnson. There had been several cases recently which were similar to ours, and in each case the Federal court had directed that Negroes be admitted to institutions of learning exclusively for whites, unless equivalent facilities and opportunities were otherwise provided within the state. After hearing all the evidence, Judge Ford directed the officials of the University to admit Johnson.

I received a letter from Assistant Attorney General Holifield stating that in spite of our longtime friendship, if I permitted a Negro to enter the University, he would be compelled under the Day Law to prosecute me. He insisted that Judge Ford's directive in no way changed the legality of the Day Law. This message disturbed me greatly. I found myself in a no man's land between the State courts threatening me with prosecution if I admitted a Negro, and a Federal court directing me to open the door to Negroes. When I made a call on Judge Ford, he informed me that Mr. Holifield was correct and that the legality of the Day Law had been in no way changed by the Federal judge's words. He added, however, that if I were threatened with prosecution, I could come into his court and seek protection until the question of the legality of the Day Law could be determined.

At the next meeting of the Board of Trustees I reported the action of the United States District Court and recommended that we admit qualified Negroes to the University and not appeal the case to the United States Supreme Court, as this would cause much delay and cost the University a considerable sum of money. I had scarcely completed my recommendation when a storm broke out in the meeting. Twelve of the fifteen members of the Board were present, and they were about equally divided in their views. I was shocked at the deep emotions brought forth by this issue. Men who had always been serene, cool, and deliberate in their meetings became excited, vehement, and explosive. They forgot parliamentary procedures. Frequently several of them talked at the same time. The Governor insisted that my recommendation be approved. Judge C. E. O'Rear, leader of the opposition, demanded that we appeal the decision to the Supreme Court. After a long and violent debate, the question was put to a vote. Five trustees voted to accept my recommendation to admit Negroes, seven voted against it. This was the first time I had ever had a recommendation to the Board turned down. However, this vote did not end the controversy.

Before the emotions died down, Judge O'Rear stood and addressed the chair formally. He pulled out of his coat pocket a paper that had been carefully prepared before the meeting, in which he memorialized the Governor in a resolution to issue immediately a call for an extraordinary session of the legislature for the purpose of appropriating funds for the building and maintenance of a university for Negroes equal in every respect to the University of Kentucky. He then proceeded to give his reasons why this should be done. His oration appeared to irritate the Governor. Finally he, too, rose to his feet, and in anger accused Judge O'Rear of playing politics. The two men exchanged heated remarks from the opposite ends of the long table separating them by about twenty feet. The air was very tense; it seemed as if the two men might come to blows.

At this point in the argument, Judge Stoll, a member of the Board for a good fifty years, very quietly and with great dignity took charge. He said that he had been opposed to the admission of Negroes to the University and that he had voted against my recommendation. He requested the trustees to reconsider the motion in calmness and without prejudice. He said that he had observed that when the trustees followed the President's recommendations, they seldom made a mistake. He added that since he had voted to kill the motion to accept my recommendation, he desired now to change his vote from *no* to *yes*. At this point in the discussion Trustee R. P. Hobson moved that the question be reconsidered. The rollcall vote on this motion showed ten votes for the President's recommendation and two against it. The motion was declared adopted, and the University announced that the case would not be appealed to the Supreme Court. At the opening of the summer term, in June, 1949, Negroes were accepted as students in the Graduate School of the University for the first time. Thirty students were admitted.

The policy followed by the University after Judge Ford's decision was to admit Negroes to the Graduate School and the professional schools whenever they had exhausted all opportunities available in their chosen fields of study at the Kentucky State College at Frankfort. This policy was followed until the Supreme Court made its decision on integration in 1954 and thus invalidated the Day Law. Since that date, Negro students have been admitted to the University on the same basis as white students.

I have never done a more careful bit of soul searching than

when I sought to discover a few fundamental policies to guide us in administering this delicate program. We knew that one mistake might result in wounds that would require years to heal. My first principle was that the integration program should be one of gradualism. The second was that there would be no announced rules or restrictions upon which the press could seize. We thought it best not to roll out the red carpet and welcome our new students with a lot of fanfare. Instead, we decided to receive them without giving any publicity to their coming.

The next step was to prepare the faculty and staff for the innovation. Some of them had been brought up in the atmosphere of the Old South. On the other hand, there were professors who wanted to demonstrate their zeal over the coming of the new order. It was no easy matter to strike a balance between these two extremes. Upon several occasions the University Faculty discussed this subject. It was surprising how readily the program was given general acceptance by the faculty and staff.

It was agreed that on admission the dean of men would interview each Negro man, and the dean of women each Negro woman, on problems of living and conduct that might call for adjustment. It was agreed also that the dean of each college would interview personally each Negro enrolling in his college in regard to his relations with white students in his classes. We pointed out that we wanted integration to succeed, and that if it were to succeed without unpleasant incidents, we must move into it slowly and unostentatiously, the less publicity the better. We requested cooperation of Negro students in a few simple things: that they sit together in the classroom rather than scatter over the room, that when they entered the cafeteria, they sit at a table with their fellow Negro students instead of each occupying a separate table. We advised them never to go to a table where white students were already seated, but that if white students on their own initiative came and sat with them, they should feel at ease. Somewhat to our surprise, this was exactly what happened; white students on frequent occasions joined Negro students at their table. We asked the Negroes not to go to the Student Union for the first year of this experiment and to keep away from social programs. We told them to find their own living quarters and to work out their own social life with their own people. Several years passed before a Negro was assigned to a room in one of the dormitories. After the first year, we leaked out the word to them that it made no difference where they sat in classrooms or cafeteria, and that it was all right for them to go to the Student Union Building.

When white students were asked what they thought about Negroes entering the University, their reply was most often, "Why not?" From the first admission of Negroes to the University to the present time, there has been no incident that has embarrassed either them or the white students. The conduct of the Negro students has been exemplary. They have gone about their business quietly and with dignity. They have not displayed any evidence of exultation over their victory in gaining entrance to the University, nor have they shown any spirit of braggadocio. The white students have for the most part ignored their presence; however, this is not to imply that they have been antagonistic or unkind.

The number of Negroes enrolled in the University during any single term has been less than one hundred, even in the summer sessions, and most of these have been graduate students engaged in teaching. In discussing the future enrollment of Negroes in the University, President R. B. Atwood of Kentucky State College said, "I do not believe the University of Kentucky will ever have a large enrollment of our people. Most of them do not want to go to the University; they would much rather be in college with their own people. What they wanted was the right to go to the University."

It is only fair to say that our program of integration was quite simple as compared with that in Alabama, Georgia, Mississippi, South Carolina, and other southern states. In Kentucky, less than 8 percent of the population are Negroes. It would not have been so easy for us if 40 percent of our population had been Negroes.

It is my considered judgment that the people of the Deep South must be given plenty of time, if integration is to be attained without great bitterness, riots, and possible bloodshed. There should be a deliberate program of gradualism. Time is a great solver of problems. Let us be willing to accept small gains so long as there is progress.

CHAPTER TWELVE

The Athletics Program of the University

THE University has had an athletics programs since about 1890. However, it was for many years a very informal program, largely directed by the students interested in sports. Its first professionally trained coach was John A. Thompson, who served as early as 1893. The students at that time had to purchase their own uniforms and such equipment as was necessary to play the games. The institution put no money into the program and took very little interest in its management and control.

There were but few rules and regulations. The story is told that in one of the early football games several of the University's players were injured and there were no more substitutes to take their places. "Time out" was called, and the opponents agreed to permit our coach to play in the place of one of the injured men. When playing out-of-state teams, it was not uncommon for our team to borrow good athletes from other colleges to help us out. Such practices were not forbidden, since there were no athletic conferences to provide controls. All was fair in war—and athletics. In time, athletic conferences were organized, rules of the game were agreed upon, and these rules were codified, though they were not always observed.

Irregularities were difficult to prove in the old days because there were no enforcement agencies such as we have today, when such conferences as the Big Ten, the Southeastern, the Pacific Coast, the Southwest, the Atlantic Coast, and the Missouri Valley set up commissioners who employ well-trained detectives to investigate violation of conferences rules and punish the offenders severely. On top of the regional conference is the National Collegiate Athletics Association, a strong, well-administered organization with sufficient authority to discipline any institution, big or little, for the violation of accepted rules and regulations. The authority of this organization can go so far as to prohibit a college or university from participating in athletics for a period of time, or it may impose a fine upon an institution for violations.

As a result of these reforms, the athletic programs of educational institutions are carried out today on a higher ethical plane than they were twenty years ago. These highly efficient organizations to control athletics may have destroyed to a degree the spirit of amateurism in colleges, but it is certain that they have done much to eliminate cheating and to promote fair play and honesty.

Football in the early days was a rough-and-tumble affair, the outcome depending more on brutal strength than on skill and and generalship. Usually an interested professor helped the boys by coaching them on such fundamentals as he knew. His reward was—nearly always—the personal satisfaction he got out of it. The University of Kentucky in 1898 developed a team commonly referred to, even up to this day, as "The Immortals," because they did not lose a game during the entire season. These "Immortals" would probably make a poor showing against any well-coached varsity team today.

College football at the University of Kentucky, prior to the close of World War II, was never properly financed. From time to time we had good teams, but seldom a great team. Good coaches were sacrificed to the "wolves" who demanded champions without providing the means to keep pace with our competitors, who recruited the best players in our region and frequently in the nation.

Shortly after my appointment as President of the University in the fall of 1941, the Lexington Chamber of Commerce gave a dinner in my honor, welcoming me to Lexington. At that dinner my classmate of the class of 1914, Guy Huguelet, asked me what kind of football team I was going to support at the University. My answer was that I would support the coaches in their efforts to have as good a team as some of the best teams in the Southeastern Conference, and that over a period of years we would win our share of championships. Within a few weeks after I made this promise, World War II was upon us. All our effort was turned to the winning of the war.

After the close of hostilities, our attention was again turned to a consideration of the athletics program of the University. There was an insistent demand throughout the State that a better athletics program should be provided for the University. This demand came from businessmen, professional men, farmers, and even laborers. When I appeared before a Joint Committee on Appropriations of the General Assembly, they listened to me politely for the twenty minutes allotted to me. When my time had elapsed, I stopped, but they told me to go on. Then I talked for an hour, telling them how the University had been neglected and how important it was to the State that its University be properly sustained. As I closed my remarks, I said that I would be glad to answer questions that any member of the committtee might desire to ask me. Immediately a State senator shot this question at me: "When are you going to have a great football team at the University?" All that I had said about the need of the University was ignored. For the next half hour I listened to these legislators telling me that the outstanding need of the University was a great football team. These men of affairs who approved the budget of the State convinced me that the University would not receive proper support if we continued to ignore the athletics program. From that day forth, I determined that our athletics program should be as good as the program of the upper half of the universities in our conference. I accepted this policy because it seemed

THE ATHLETICS PROGRAM OF THE UNIVERSITY

the best way to enlist the support of the majority of our citizens for our educational program. The policy has paid off. The University has continuously received larger appropriations for its total educational program.

Some months after this experience with the legislators, I invited thirty-six prominent citizens of Lexington who were known to be interested in athletics, and especially in football, to lunch with me. That day, December 15, 1945, I told them that we were ready to launch a better athletics program at the University, provided that the public would "foot the bill." I said that he who dances must pay the piper, and that the sports lover who enjoyed the game would have to provide the cash to support the program. I stated that I was opposed to an athletics program to entertain the public at State expense, and that not one dollar of tax money was to go into the support of our athletics. I told these gentlemen that we would not launch this program until we raised $100,000 and had it in the bank against "a rainy day." They immediately accepted the challenge, and before we adjourned, they had pledged $33,000. An organization was formed, committees were selected to make the solicitation, and the campaign was on. Within a few weeks our goal was reached, and before we closed our campaign, we had collected $113,000.

This money was deposited in the account of the University of Kentucky Athletic Association; later it was invested in United States government bonds, to be used only in the event that we should have a disastrous season. The complete fund is still intact. It is to be used only in a real emergency.

At a meeting of the Executive Committee of the Board of Trustees on November 17, 1945, I presented, and the Committee approved, Articles of Incorporation for the University of Kentucky Athletic Association. I then submitted an agreement between this University of Kentucky Athletic Association and the Board of Trustees. This agreement had previously been studied and approved by the attorney general of Kentucky. The trustees unanimously approved this agreement, which then was signed by Judge Stoll, chairman of the Executive Committee of the Board of Trustees of the University of Kentucky (party of the first part) and by H. L. Donovan as president of the University of Kentucky Athletic Association (party of the second part). Copies of the Articles of Incorporation and of the Articles of Agreement are printed in full in Appendix B.

By this arrangement the athletics program of the University was placed under control of a board of directors of the independent University of Kentucky Athletic Association. This board consisted of the President of the University and ten other members, five of whom were faculty members, one an alumnus, one a trustee, and one the president of the Student Government Association. There was no possible way by which the alumni or any other group could take over control of our athletics.

Why did the University resort to such unusual procedure? First, because the constitutional salary limit of that time, $5,000 a year, made it impossible for the University to secure a competent coach. Second, because there had long been a fear that some outside group, possibly even the alumni, might come to dominate the management of the University's athletics activities. Third, because certain State laws and administrative regulations made it impossible to operate effectively, especially in regard to such points as securing permission of the State commissioner of finance for a team's out-of-state travel, the purchase of equipment, the holding of athletics funds in the State treasury, delays in purchasing emergency needs, and other petty details. We concluded that no athletics program that moved on a time schedule was possible under so many handicaps; so we turned to the device of incorporating an Athletic Association that would do a better job than could be done under archaic regulations and laws from the State capital.

In addition to supporting our football and basketball programs, the Association has carried on a program of so-called minor sports, including swimming, golf, track, tennis, baseball, fencing, and rifle. In addition, it has subsidized the intramural program in a substantial way, building tennis courts, handball courts, and a practice football field. It has purchased thousands of dollars worth of athletic equipment, carried a bond issue on the Coliseum amounting to $885,000 and a bond issue on the Stadium for $300,000, paying the interest on the same and amortizing these debts.

The Association pays the salaries of all coaches and all other employees engaged in any capacity in the athletics program of the University. It has also purchased uniforms for the marching band, and pays the expenses of their out-of-town trips. Financially, it is a sound, well-managed organization under the supervision of a director, who in turn reports to the Vice President of the University and to the Athletic Association. The tale of the University of Kentucky Athletic Association is a great success story. It has paid all the expenses of a splendid athletics program. The sports-loving public has relieved the taxpayers of this burden by picking up the check for this activity of the University.

Assessing the state of affairs up to the time the Athletic Association was formed (1945), we find that the general public was well pleased with the basketball program. Coach Adolph Rupp had been highly successful in producing outstanding basketball teams from the very beginning of his coaching career at the University in 1930-1931. He had won 85 percent of his games, and was regarded by most of the sportswriters as the "nation's winningest basketball coach." With the results in football, the general public was far from happy. Bitter complaints were constantly being received at the President's office; the trustees were under pressure to do something about our poor showing. The Governors of the State and members of the General Assembly for many years lectured the President on our poor record in football and demanded action on our part. The coaches were able men, but they were the victims of a poorly financed athletics program. We had many good players, but not enough reserves to win many games. As a result, we were practically always in the lower half in our conference at the end of the season.

The members of the board of the Athletic Association asked the President and the director to make a nationwide search for a football coach, authorizing us to pay the new coach $10,000 a year instead of the previous salary of $5,000. Finally we secured Coach Paul Bryant—personable, dynamic, ambitious, and determined—a great coach. During the eight years he stayed with us, Kentucky participated in four postseason games: Great Lakes, Orange, Sugar, and Cotton bowls. We won three out of the four in which we played. Coach Bryant lifted the University from the football cellar in which we had so long dwelt. When Mr. Bryant left this institution to accept a coaching position at Texas A. and M., many of our football fans, as well as the members of the athletics board, deplored his departure.

Soon we secured the services of Blanton Collier, who had been with the Cleveland Browns as assistant coach for some years. He maintained the same high standard in football that prevailed in Bryant's regime. He proved himself a great leader of men, interested in the character and intellectual abilities of the boys as well as in their athletic achievement.

In discussing the athletics program of the University, I believe that I should express my personal views of the objectives of such a program in a state university of medium size such as the University of Kentucky represents. We are a typical State University, designed to serve all the people of the State through its educational and research programs. The members of the Board of Trustees have a pretty good idea of what the people want, and they are usually vocal in expressing these views. One thing the citizens want, they say, is that the University should maintain a good athletics program; nothing second-rate will satisfy them. They say that our people are sports-minded; the newspapers, the radio, and television have educated them to be so. These same organs of communication frequently denounce institutions for overemphasis in athletics while daily building up in us great sports interest through their sportswriters and telecasters. It does not take much effort to overstimulate interest in this field.

I believe that state universities, as well as many other colleges, find it imperative to provide an athletics program in all the sports where there is a compelling interest. The program should be held within reason, and here is where the president, the faculty, and the athletics board must use discretion. It is not easy to maintain a balanced program of athletics. The president is constantly bombarded by the sports fans for more and better athletics on the one hand, while at the same time he is under pressure from the intellectuals to deemphasize the program. It takes courage to strike a happy medium. Ideally there should be a sports program that would attract the interest of every student enrolled in the institution, but the average citizen is indifferent to all sports but football and basketball. A wise administration will capitalize on the interest of the sports fans and charge them admission fees to the games in the major sports sufficient to carry the program of the minor sports and to aid the intramural program. It is my personal opinion that every student in a university should participate in some sport that will give him exercise. If that sport is one that can be carried over into adult life after college years are over, so much the better. The University of Kentucky, under the Athletic Association, has endeavored to work toward this end.

I believe that an athlete who excels in some sports should be considered for financial aid the same as an excellent debater, a first-class musician, or a brilliant student in the academic subjects; but an athletic scholarship should not be awarded to a young man unless he has sufficient ability to do college work. The amount of time required to take part in football or basketball of the quality played in most of our universities today is excessive, and not many young men meet the requirements demanded of them by the coaches and at the same time make superior marks. At the University our policy has been that an athlete must stay off probation if he is to stay on the team.

The Southeastern Conference showed wisdom some years ago when it set up a policy of awarding grants-in-aid to outstanding athletes. The maximum number of scholarships in each sport was determined by the conference. At the time this action was taken, there was widespread criticism of this program, but with the passing of the years, other conferences have gradually accepted this policy, or at least some modification of it. Today the policy of awarding athletes financial assistance prevails throughout the nation. Before this policy came into general acceptance, most colleges and universities gave jobs to athletes to meet their expenses. This was an artifice, a subterfuge. If made-up jobs were not available, many universities permitted wealthy alumni to subsidize outstanding athletes by an evasion of the rules in a practice commonly called "under-the-table aid." This was gross dishonesty, a corruption of the morals of the youth who was awarded such aid. Our Athletic Association would disqualify a player receiving such aid and report the case to the Southeastern Conference if it were called to our attention.

We believe that the best way to keep athletics clean is to have regional conferences administered by men of ability and character, men whose integrity is unquestioned, men who will enforce rules as objectively as a judge in our courts. These men should have the authority to punish an institution for infraction of standards, suspend an athlete for violation of rules, and even disqualify a coach for unethical practices. I am also with the National Collegiate Athletics Association in its endeavor to police athletics on a national level. It should be a supreme court to which a college or university could appeal if it felt that it had been unjustly treated by regional conferences. If a regional conference should fail to act on irregularities within its region, the NCAA should not hesitate to investigate and to act on its findings.

After twenty-eight years as a college president, it is my considerate judgment that no other activity of a college or university is as difficult to administer as the athletics program.

THE ATHLETICS PROGRAM OF THE UNIVERSITY 111

Unfortunately, more people have an interest in athletics than in education, and in their desire to have a winning team, they sometimes do things that disrupt an institution. There are gamblers who will bribe coaches and players if they can. There are others who put so much pressure on both coaches and players that they make life miserable. There are many alumni who demand that the coach produce winning teams every year or be "fired." This overemphasis on athletics is unwholesome and makes many problems for the administration and faculty of an institution. I wish I could prescribe some formula that would solve the problem of overemphasis. Some universities, such as Chicago and Emory, have abolished competitive athletics, but that does not solve the problem even locally. Athletics are good for students when kept within reason. The general public demands of state universities an athletics program of high quality; not a state university in the country has yet had the courage to deny this demand. It is my observation that a good, clean, effective athletics program is one of the best approaches to good public relations. It appears to be the one program of the university that all people, high and low, can understand and appreciate.

Some years ago, just after the basketball scandals had occurred, the American Council on Education appointed a committee of distinguished university presidents to consider athletics of educational institutions with a view to the deemphasis of sports. This committee made an earnest effort and brought forth an excellent report. Two of the best friends I have ever had were on this committee, President John A. Hannah of Michigan State University and Chancellor John D. Williams of the University of Mississippi. Dr. Hannah was chairman of the committee. Within a year or two after the committee had reported, Michigan State played in the Rose Bowl and Mississippi in the Sugar Bowl.

While the committee was still considering the problems assigned to it, I had the pleasure of riding with Chancellor Williams from Oxford, Mississippi, to Gulfport, to attend a meeting of the Southern University Conference—and back by a different route. Every time we stopped at a gas station, restaurant, drugstore, or hotel, the attendant who served us would inquire of Chancellor Williams about the kind of football "Ole Miss" would have that fall. This was practically the only subject discussed by the citizens of Mississippi in their contact with the distinguished chancellor of their university. Needless to say, I was greatly amused by these conversations. I had much fun at the expense of my friend when I insisted that he outline to me his program of deemphasis. Does anyone think that the public would let either Michigan State or Mississippi deemphasize its athletics program?

In the fall of 1951 news flashed like a bolt of lightning from a blue sky that two of our former Olympic basketball players, members of the "Fabulous Five" (1945-1949), had been arrested on the charge of accepting bribes to control point spreads in basketball games. Weeks before this time, we had heard that players from some other prominent colleges had been similarly charged. At this time none of us at the University felt the slightest fear that any of our players would be found to be implicated in the spreading scandal. Coach Rupp had said, "The gamblers couldn't touch our boys with a ten-foot pole!" Yet soon six members of our squad were involved.

When the press called me for a statement, I said, "We have great confidence in the integrity of these young men, and the news that they accepted a bribe to fix a game is difficult for us to believe. There is no doubt in our minds that these were good boys; but were inexperienced when it came to dealing with gamblers."

The story, as I have been able to piece it together, is this: The gamblers enticed our players in some such way as saying that if the boys could beat X university by eighteen points or more, they would give each of them $100. They knew that this pay incentive would cause the players to double their efforts, and they, the gamblers, dared to bet on a point spread higher than that published by the bookmakers. When the gamblers thought the players were conditioned to a reversal, they proposed that the boys make a smaller number of points than the published point spread. This was a violation of the law of several states, including New York. If they could win the game and yet maintain the specified point spread, the boys were each to be paid $500. This arrangement made it very profitable for the gamblers, for then they were betting with the bookmakers and others on a sure thing. It was a diabolical device by which the gamblers had the players under their control.

These were inexperienced young college boys who were no match for gamblers and racketeers, who by their slick and adroit scheme subtly bribed and victimized naive boys. These boys were no match for syndicated crooks.

I am not condoning the acts of our former basketball players. They had to accept the responsibilities that went with their misdeeds. I believe that they have suffered mental anguish. They should not be forever damned for the mistakes that they made. They have paid dearly for these mistakes. The University has forgiven them of their sins; I trust that society will likewise forgive and try to forget their tragic experience.

I have done much soul searching to determine what mistakes we at the University, especially the administration and the athletics staff, made that led to the basketball scandal. Did we overemphasize our athletics program? Many people believe we did; some newspapers and radio and television stations charged us with overemphasis while at the same time they stepped up their reports on athletics, stimulating the public to become more and more interested in all college sports. If we were overemphasizing athletics at the University of Kentucky, we were only keeping in step with an overwhelming majority of the great American universities. Maybe there was overemphasis in athletics everywhere! Inquire of Mr. Citizen and find out what he says about it.

One mistake we made, I am certain. It was made when we accepted invitations to play basketball games in Madison Square Garden, in the environment of which unscrupulous gamblers operated and racketeering prevailed. College athletic contests should be scheduled on college campuses, in their own gymnasiums, fieldhouses, coliseums, and stadiums. Much of the temptation to which players have been subjected has come from the environment in big cities over which a university has no control. I am convinced that there would never have been a basketball scandal at the University of Kentucky if we had followed this policy.

As soon as we learned that some of our players were charged with accepting bribes to shave points in basketball games in New York, we pledged the district attorney our cooperation in ferreting out the facts in the case. Governor Lawrence Wetherby and I both invited him to come to Lexington to make a careful investigation and promised our wholehearted support in his effort to clean up the scandal. When the assistant district attorney, Mr. Vincent O'Conner, came to Lexington we found him to be a gentleman in every respect: fair and honest, highly intelligent, but at the same time determined to break up gambling and bribetaking in collegiate athletics. We found not a scintilla of evidence to connect Mr. Rupp or any other employee of the University with the bribery. Later, when three of the players implicated in the scandal confessed every detail of the arrangements, they completely exonerated Coach Rupp and all local persons of any connection.

While the district attorney deplored the behavior of the players and recognized that they must be punished for their misdeeds, his attitude toward them was much more kind than it was toward the gamblers found to be involved, all of whom were sent to prison. If a player confessed honestly his implication, the district attorney recommended to the court that he be given a suspended sentence. Of the six players implicated, five pleaded guilty and received a suspended sentence; one denied his guilt and was tried in Judge Saul S. Streit's court, where the result was a hung jury and later dismissal of the charge. The judge issued a 45-page tirade on college sports, indicting institutions from the Great Lakes to the Gulf of Mexico and

THE ATHLETICS PROGRAM OF THE UNIVERSITY 115

from New York to California, recklessly charging them with infractions of the rules, and often making unwarranted statements that did untold harm to the reputation of many distinguished institutions. He unjustly implied a connection between Coach Rupp and the gamblers. In his distorted picture of the athletics program at the University of Kentucky, he made a public denunciation of the University, its trustees, its administrative officials, its faculty, its alumni, its coaches, and even the community of Lexington. He said not a word about his own bailiwick, from whence came the gamblers who bribed the players of a number of colleges.

We requested the officials of the Southeastern Conference and the National Collegiate Athletics Association to make a thorough investigation of the charges, and promised them our complete cooperation. Both of these organizations sent investigators and called executive committee meetings. Eventually the Southeastern Conference passed the verdict that the University of Kentucky be suspended from playing basketball for one year.

We soon recognized that the nation, through the press, was clamoring for a victim whose punishment might wash our common sins away. Even college people wanted to believe that the humiliation of one well-known university would cleanse all colleges and universities. When we saw that we were making no progress and that the executive committee of the Southeastern Conference was going to stand by its decision, Dr. A. D. Kirwan, faculty chairman of athletics at the University, rose and made one of the most eloquent speeches I have ever heard. Having been a coach for a number of years at the University, he was well aware of the violations of rules and regulations which many of the coaches in the Southeastern Conference had committed. He began to catalog violations by the members, pointing out one after another, giving the names of institutions, the names of coaches, the time and place of violations. It was a long list, and many of the offenses were major in character. Many of these violations were in the universities whose presidents were sitting in judgment on our case. Not a man on the committee dared to deny the charges recited by Dr. Kirwan.

Presently the executive committee of the National Collegiate Athletics Association recommended suspension for the 1952-1953 season. Officials of the University protested that this suspension did harm to the team for 1952-1953, since all the members of this team were innocent of any wrongdoing in the affair and yet were the players actually being penalized for the offense. They likewise protested the unfairness of a penalty which was equivalent to a fine of $100,000, as our income from basketball games had for many years yielded more than this amount. We expected the guilty boys to be punished, but we never expected that innocent boys would suffer and that the University would be fined with a verdict of such astronomical proportions. Our protests were entirely unavailing.

The involvement of our basketball team in the athletics scandal was the greatest humiliation we have ever experienced. The trustees, the administration, the faculty, the alumni, and the students were embarrassed. But in this humiliation, we determined that so far as the University of Kentucky was concerned, nothing like this would ever happen again. Philosophically we have accepted our punishment in fines and humiliation. We have come to the conclusion that the regional conferences and the NCAA are essential organizations for the control of athletics programs in this country. It is our wish, much as we have suffered from their rulings, that they may ever be vigilant in the enforcement of their regulations.

It is easy to see why I hold that the most trying problem of a college administrator is the athletics program.

CHAPTER THIRTEEN

The University's Library Facilities

*I*N 1907 Andrew Carnegie, a good friend of President James K. Patterson, gave the University $26,500 for the construction of a modest library building. Prior to this date, collections of books were to be found in some departments on the campus, but they could scarcely be said to constitute a University library. The number of books in these collections did not exceed 15,000 volumes, and their value was about $22,000. The Carnegie Library was officially dedicated on November 24, 1909. There were but few books in it at that time and it grew slowly for a number of years. The Carnegie Building is now the Museum of Anthropology.

When President McVey came to the University in 1917, he reported that the library contained 36,201 volumes. Twenty-four years later in his last annual report, 1941, he said with pride that the library had 260,000 volumes and a large number of pamphlets, cards, and materials of other kinds. An increase of 600 percent in 24 years is due cause for pride.

The Carnegie Building soon proved to be too small to house the rapid accession of books and the increasing attendance of students. A much larger building had to be erected to accommodate the growing institution. In 1929 the money with which to construct a new library became available, coming from the inheritance tax on the estate of Mrs. Robert Bingham. The tax laws of Kentucky at that time provided that a certain percentage of the inheritance taxes collected by the State should go to the University of Kentucky, and it was with this money, amounting to approximately $450,000, that the new library was constructed. This building was dedicated on October 23, 1931. This library was later named the Margaret I. King Library in honor of Miss King, who served as the University's first professional librarian from 1910 until she was given a change of work in 1949. The erection of this library, together with the acquisition of more than a quarter of a million books, was regarded by Dr. McVey as one of the outstanding accomplishments of his term as President of the University of Kentucky.

No university can achieve greatness unless it has a great library. Books are the tools that a student must have at hand if he is to secure a good education. Firmly convinced of this idea, I continued the McVey policy of increasing the usefulness of the library by almost doubling its collection of books during the fifteen years of my presidency. At the time of my retirement, September 1, 1956, the library contained 712,612 cataloged volumes, and in addition, 1,125,151 pamphlets, manuscripts, cards, and similar items. This represents an increase of 175 percent in my administration.

The library of the University of Kentucky now ranks as the fourth or fifth largest library in the South. It is one of the forty-nine members of the Association of Research Libraries, a select group of the leading American libraries. Its shelves are filled from basement to attic, and the problem of the library staff is how to crowd another volume into this building. In 1951, when the University was erecting a new Service Building, the trustees decided to add an additional floor to the original design to provide for the storage of valuable books and manuscripts seldom used. Today the fourth floor of the Service Building houses many thousands of books and other collections, and there is little space left for expansion.

One of the most acute problems that the University faces, as I see it, is the growing need for more library space to house books, and the necessary staff to accommodate the rising tide

THE UNIVERSITY'S LIBRARY FACILITIES 119

of registered students. Only half of the library as planned in 1929 had been erected; the other half should be built now. One of the disappointments in the years of my presidency was my failure to enlarge the library building. That is one of my dreams that did not come true.

The number of library staff members employed in 1941-1942 was 22; the number employed in 1956-1957 was 54. The budget of the library in 1941-1942 was $79,477; the budget for 1956-1957 was $324,362.

For more than fifty years generous friends of the library have been giving rare books and manuscripts to the University. One of the first of these outstanding gifts came from President Patterson, who left his entire library to the University, a valuable collection. Since 1941, a number of important collections have been given. In 1946 the late Judge Samuel Wilson bequeathed to the University his library of several thousand books, many of them very rare and precious. The McVey papers have been given by his children to the library. The Anderson, Griffith, and Hammer collections lend distinction to the library as a graphic-arts center. In 1944 Mrs. Stuart Chevalier, a descendant of the University's second President, gave to the library the excellent collection of her grandfather and father. A distinguished collection of Canadiana is being built up through the generous gifts of Lawrence M. Wilson of Montreal. W. Hugh Peal of New York is doing much to strengthen collections in English literature. Norman Shouse of New York has contributed many choice examples of fine printing.

At the present time a very significant accession is the Henry Clay Papers, mainly photographic copies, that are being assembled by Dr. James F. Hopkins.

A recent loan and gift of great value has come from Mrs. Alben Barkley and Senator Barkley's children. As early as 1942 Senator Barkley was approached relative to leaving his state papers with the library of the University. This request was repeated from time to time. Dr. Bennett Wall had kept before the Senator the importance of placing his letters, manuscripts, speeches, and reports in the library of his State's University for the benefit of future generations. The gift of Mrs. Barkley and the Barkley children was the ultimate result. Mrs. Barkley also deposited with the library the Senator's trophies, his gavels, his desk and office chair, and memorabilia of great value. At present the collection is being cataloged for display in a Barkley Room in the library, dedicated to the memory of a great statesman who was a native son of Kentucky.

Gifts such as the Wilson Library and the Barkley Papers are among the high points in an aggressive acquisition policy inspired for a quarter of a century by Professor Thomas D. Clark, head of the History Department of the University of Kentucky. It would be safe to say that since Lyman Draper, no collector of historical source material has a solid record of achievement comparable to that of Tom Clark.

Some twenty years ago, when Professor Ezra L Gillis reached the age of seventy and was required to take a change of work under the rules of the University, he requested President McVey to permit him to continue working full time at a reduced salary. At that time (1937) he set about the organization of the Bureau of Source Materials in Higher Education in the library. Since then, he has been collecting a wealth of data about the University of Kentucky and other Kentucky colleges. His collection includes also school records, public documents, correspondence of distinguished citizens, textbooks, manuscripts, and scores of other records of great value to future historians and other writers seeking material on Kentucky and its schools and colleges. The collection now is one of great magnitude and inestimable value.

When Miss King was given a change of assignment in the late 1940's, a diligent search was made for a young man to head the library organization of the University. After a nationwide canvass, Dr. Lawrence S. Thompson was employed as director of libraries. He was placed in charge of both the main library and of the departmental and collegiate libraries that had not formerly been under the supervision of the chief librarian.

THE UNIVERSITY'S LIBRARY FACILITIES 121

Prior to Dr. Thompson's appointment, there had been little integration between the departmental libraries and the main collection. In recent years the number of departmental libraries has been reduced, especially through their combination into divisional libraries. For example, in the case of the biological sciences and the fine arts, several libraries that had been combined could thereafter be served by a full-time staff.

In his 1955-1956 annual report to the President, Dr. Thompson lists some of the positive achievements since 1941:

1. Doubling of total holdings.
2. Rising curve of statistics of use.
3. Acquisition of several notable collections.
4. Development of Department of Archives and Special Collections.
5. Development of Photographic Service, and program of filming Kentucky newspapers.
6. Beginning of program of manuscript collecting.
7. Restricted policy on opening new departmental libraries.
8. Use of Library Annex in Service Building, to relieve pressure.
9. Organization of the Library Associates.

The administration of the libraries of the University is under the director of libraries. There is a Library Committee composed of fifteen professors representing the various colleges and schools, to formulate policies and advise with the director from time to time. The director of libraries reports directly to Vice President Leo M. Chamberlain, who has contributed much to building up the library.

CHAPTER FOURTEEN

The University Press and Foundations

*I*N 1943 the Board of Trustees authorized the establishment of the University of Kentucky Press. The Press is maintained by an annual grant from the Haggin Fund, an appropriation from the general fund of the University, and the revenue derived from the sale of books.

The director of the Press is Bruce F. Denbo, who has proved to be a dynamic leader in this field. A committee of the faculty appointed by the President serves in an advisory capacity to the director in the formation of policies of the Press and in the selection of manuscripts for publication.

The Press is dedicated to the publication of scholarly books. In its short period of operation it has published more than forty titles. Many of these books have been written by our professors, and the establishment of the Press has stimulated faculty research and scholarly writing.

The recognition which the University of Kentucky Press has attained during its short history has been the source of much pride and great satisfaction to the faculty and staff. It ranks high among the significant achievements of the University during this period.

The Kentucky Research Foundation was the outgrowth of several years of study by a committee on research appointed by President McVey. The Foundation was incorporated under the laws of Kentucky in 1945. The objectives of the Foundation are well formulated in a brochure, 1945, announcing its organization. This booklet states that such a Foundation may perform certain functions difficult or impossible for the University to perform, but which are part of the service which the State and society expect the University to render. It suggests further that "in the minds of many donors, such a Foundation offers a more satisfactory medium for the administration of a gift than does a publicly controlled institution."

In setting forth the field of this Foundation, the brochure offers the alumni and other friends of the University "opportunity to assist in the promotion of research, creative scholarship, and public service, and to encourage attendance at college on the part of worthy boys and girls who could not finance their advanced study without assistance." In another paragraph the booklet says that it is the aim of this Foundation "to act as the agent of the University in the solicitation of and administration of funds for a variety of purposes: research, public service, scholarships and fellowships, publications, the endowment of professorships, the provision of new buildings and equipment, and any other purpose consistent with the institution's governing regulations and policies."

Since its founding, the Foundation has sponsored 105 separate research grants or contracts involving expenditures of $1,937,474, as shown by the twelfth annual report of this Foundation, 1956-1957. Many of the projects have dealt with vital problems relating to our national defense in the fields of chemistry, physics, and engineering. Industry has also utilized our resources to find the answer to problems upon which the Foundation and the faculty were prepared to lend assistance.

Many of our professors have been greatly stimulated by the opportunities to carry on research that they would never have been able to undertake if the Foundation had not been organized, and if it had not provided guidance and assistance in obtaining the contracts. Some of the Foundation projects have involved only small sums of money; others have run into many thousands of dollars. Some have been completed in a few months; others have run for several years. Payments for overhead above the actual cost of the projects are accumulated to provide further support for basic research and to make available scholarships and fellowships for needy and brilliant students to continue their education and prepare for greater service to society. The Foundation has been able to grant 536 scholarships, and the number is increasing each year.

Some endowment funds have been established for the support of scholarships and have been assigned to the Foundation to administer. These endowments serve as memorials to donors or to other persons. The following represent gifts of this kind:

Endowment	Amount
Frances Jewell McVey	$25,762.00
Fannie L. Jones	7,996.00
William S. Taylor	7,791.00
Ralph McCracken	10,000.00
George Roberts	11,895.00
Juliet Shouse	6,214.00

Starting from nothing in 1945, the Kentucky Research Foundation has a general fund accumulation of $368,081.94 today. It has sponsored almost two million dollars worth of research, and it has not received a single dollar of tax money. These accomplishments, all in a period of twelve years, represent a great achievement. Much of the credit for this record belongs to Vice President Chamberlain, who has been the president of the Foundation from the beginning, and to Vice President Peterson, treasurer. They have served the Foundation without salary, as has its board of directors. The Foundation had no salaried officer until 1953, when the volume of business became so heavy that it became necessary to employ a part-time director, Dr. Merl Baker, associate professor of mechanical engineering, who has proven to be a splendid administrator.

Another significant contribution made by the Foundation to the University has been in supplementing the salaries of many of our scientists and engineers who have been carrying on various research projects. Many of these professors have been receiving from $500 to as much as $1,800 a year for the extra work they have been doing. This has enabled the University to retain some outstanding men who might otherwise have left for other teaching positions or industry.

When Dean Thomas Poe Cooper retired, many members of his faculty and staff as well as hundreds of farmers and businessmen wanted to show their appreciation of his many years of devoted service and constructive leadership given to his college, the Experiment Station, and to Agricultural Extension. Many suggestions were made to the committee set up to study the matter. Finally the committee recommended that an Agricultural Foundation be incorporated, to bear the name of Thomas Poe Cooper.

Promptly articles of incorporation were drawn up and a non-profit organization came into existence. The purposes were: to encourage scientific research in agriculture and home economics; to aid in the training of worthy young men and women for study and research in these two fields; and to encourage cooperation with other groups interested in the development of these two fields and in disseminating knowledge acquired by study and research in these fields.

The original funds donated to the Cooper Foundation were the gifts of many members of the teaching, research, and extension staffs, from farmers and businessmen who held him in high esteem, and from homemakers in all parts of Kentucky. This Foundation is now attracting the gifts of many persons who want to promote worthy agricultural enterprises, but would not make a gift directly to the University, or do not want their money mingled with public moneys. Substantial gifts to this Foundation have also been made by Kentucky Utilities, the Burley Tobacco Growers Cooperative Association and others. The total assets of the Cooper Foundation, as of June 30, 1956, were $54,130.51.

CHAPTER FIFTEEN

A University President Views Three Professions

THREE professions? Yes. Administration, teaching, and research. Take the university president first.

A timid president will be an unhappy administrator, feeling only a limited pleasure in his office. Long tenure is not to be desired at the price of compromising his ideals. College presidents have been losing their jobs ever since the first president of Harvard lost his job six years after his appointment. The average tenure of college presidents in America today is about five years. The general public is under the impression that the "dangerous" job in colleges and universities is that of coach; this is not the case, however. It is my observation that the aggressive president with a program for which he is willing to stand his ground and fight is likely to have a longer tenure than the timorous executive who worries over how to hold his office.

There are times in the life of every president when a trustee, a politician, a labor leader, or a capitalist will ask of him some favor that he cannot ethically grant. It may be the appointment of a poorly qualified teacher, or the "firing" of a so-called "radical" professor, or the suppression of a piece of research, or a denial of some professor's right to express his views on a social question related to his field of specialization. A college president must have the courage to say *no* to any demand that would compromise the integrity or the freedom of his institution. The president who does not have some fights may be a weak administrator.

What other qualities should a college president have besides the courage to stand firm in a good cause? I would place ability next, if it is coupled with intellectual interest. A strong personality, an abundance of energy, and the marks of culture will be real assets to him. He must keep books for his companions all his life. To be a good public speaker and to wield a facile pen will help him to win many a battle. He must guard the hopes and traditions of his college, and its freedom, too. Above all, he must be dedicated to his profession as a college president. The university is man's major effort to discover his universe and the part man should play in its eternal drama. The president should see to it that his institution plays its part in this drama.

What are some things I would do differently if I were to relive my career as a college president?

1. I would free myself from details that could be done by others.
2. I would travel to fewer national meetings, but would work more intensively within my own State.
3. I would make fewer and better speeches, ones that would really do justice to the office of University President.
4. I would give more personal attention to faculty and students.
5. I would give larger rewards to the great teachers who stimulate the intellectual life of the campus.
6. I would take more time to meditate about the University's work. Details have kept me from thinking profoundly about what is of greatest concern to the University.

And what shall we say about teachers and teaching? In my youth I attended a one-room school. It was taught in succession by five young women and two young men during the period of my attendance. All of these young people were kind and sympathetic, but there was not a skilled teacher among them. They were capable of receiving an education, but they had never had a chance to acquire one. They were victims of a system in which the blind led the blind, the ignorant taught the ignorant; and as a result, many an intelligent youth fell into the ditch.

We learned to read poorly, to spell only a few hundred words, to do a little figuring, to acquire a few facts of history and geography, and to write indifferently well. There was nothing to read except our textbooks. This was a typical country school threescore years ago in Kentucky. Very few of the children brought up in such country schools ever managed to reach high school. Fortunately I was one who, though poorly prepared, did enroll in high school; but my poor preparation was a handicap to me through the secondary school and even through college. Ten or more years of my childhood slipped away without the opportunity to read great books, to learn at least one other language besides my own, and to secure knowledge important to intellectual development. These were the lost years of my life that I have never been able to retrieve.

In high school the teachers were much better trained. They had attended college and had something to share with us. During this period I met my first great teacher. His name was Ezra L Gillis. He was well educated, and what was even better, he had the ability to inspire his students and to make learning attractive. All his students aspired to go to college. He lighted the lamp of learning for us. After coming under his instruction, life took on a new meaning.

While I was a student in high school, my father took me to hear the late Ollie M. James in a political address. This was the first time I had ever heard a great orator. His language was beautiful, his voice melodious. He appealed to history for his illustrations, quoted Jefferson, Clay, Lincoln, and Cleveland as if he knew them personally, and recited beautiful fragments of poetry. This master of oratory played on his audience as if he were playing on some great organ. Never before in my young life had I experienced such emotions from a speaker's words. As I listened to his eloquence, goosepimples covered my body as though I were having a chill. He did something to me that day which I have never forgotten. As we drove home that evening, my father and I spoke not a word until we were near our journey's end. Then I said, "I know what I'm going to be—a lawyer. That will give me a chance to learn to be a speaker like Ollie James." My father liked the idea and approved my choice of a profession. Later when I left for college, it was my intention to study law.

College was the greatest experience of my life up to that time. Every day was a new day full of adventure and challenge. There I became acquainted with intelligent young men and women who were on errands of the mind, and they stimulated me to do my best. I was surrounded by books, more books than I could read in a lifetime. I literally ran to my classes, then to the library, then to my room at the end of the day, where I studied until late into the night. Life and learning were very exciting; every day new vistas opened before me; I had never before realized what an interesting world this was and that I must be in haste to capture it.

Before the end of my freshman year I had changed my mind about being a lawyer. Now I knew that teaching was the profession for me. Why? Because if I became a teacher, I could live always surrounded by books and by people who loved books and learning. Then when I had acquired some learning, I could share it with others. That was my idea of teaching. That was how I became a teacher—a teacher for fifty years; for I have always regarded myself as a teacher even though I have sometimes been called principal, superintendent, dean, and even president. To me the greatest of all titles is *Teacher*. If in the next world we are given the choice of our vocation, I shall pursue the one that I followed so ardently on this earth.

Unfortunately, after two years in college, I found that I had used all my money and had exhausted my credit, and so I had to go to work. Of course I chose to teach, though I was but poorly prepared as a teacher. Later for an academic year and four summer terms I attended college again, now at the University of Kentucky, where I finally secured my baccalaureate degree. Here, too, I fell in with men of learning who were great teachers. For example, there was Professor Cotton Noe, with whom I enrolled for a class in psychology. We were required to purchase James' *Psychology* as a text and were directed to read it. But we spent all the classroom hours in reading Shakespeare. My grade on that course is recorded as a grade in psychology, but I could wish for no better course in literature. A student never forgets a scintillating professor like Dr. Edward E. Farquhar, who would say upon entering the classroom, "We are studying today Browning's *The Ring and the Book*," and then would proceed to spend the next fifty minutes reciting the poem without the benefit of a book. I remember, too, a certain memorable day long ago in Professor M. L. Pence's class in physics, when he led me to look into the future. Picking up a pitcher of water, he poured about a half pint of it into a beaker, saying that if we could separate the atoms of this water and harness them, we would have enough energy to drive the largest steamship across the ocean. Incredible! Then there was Dr. W. S. Webb, who once offered me an assistantship in physics. In his autobiography, *The Education of Henry Adams*, the author says that he never had a great teacher while he attended Harvard. I have been a student in institutions of less fame than Harvard, but have had no difficulty in identifying a number of great teachers. They are to be found in practically every college.

I deliberately planned my graduate study so as to have contact with at least three important institutions of higher education. I was seeking an experience with distinguished teachers, and I was not disappointed in my search, for I found them at Columbia, Chicago, and Peabody. They were, as teachers, own brothers of Mr. Chips. There should be greater interest on the part of the public in discovering these great teachers, in acknowledging their contribution to society, and in awarding them worthy honors for their achievements. Back of practically every great man and woman there is, in addition to a good father and mother, also a great teacher who has inspired and guided the individual.

In this country we need to recognize great teachers and reward them fittingly, for such recognition will certainly stimulate many a young man and woman to choose teaching as a profession. It may seem hard to ascertain who are the great teachers on a university faculty. The president, the deans, and the heads of departments seldom—very seldom indeed—enter classrooms and observe the teaching that is going on, as supervisors in the public schools would do. About the only way university administrators can judge good teaching is by hearing what the students say about their teachers. I have observed over many years that the group judgment of students relative to the quality of instruction is fairly accurate. This is not to say that you can take the judgment of one student, or a dozen students, and arrive at an accurate rating of a teacher's instruction. But if you have heard year after year the opinion of students on the quality of a teacher's work, that opinion is probably the best guide to his efficiency in the classroom. It is my judgment that a great deal more attention should be given to improving instruction in college classrooms than we are giving at present. What is going on in many classes under the guise of teaching is little more than a travesty of teaching.

The quality of a professor's teaching today depends entirely upon his conscience and integrity. There are no checks on his classroom performance. If he is inclined to do so, he can get by with simply meeting his classes. There should be some means devised to protect students from such malpractice, and also to shield the reputation of excellent teachers who suffer from the culpable neglect of the imposter who wraps himself in the cloak of a professor but contributes nothing to the intellectual development of his students.

And what shall we say of those who pursue research? As I look back over a half century and review the standing of the teaching profession then and now, I am inclined to believe that teachers have lost ground in the estimation of the general public and of their colleagues. The researcher and the writer have steadily gained ground—and at the expense of the teacher, I fear. Seldom do we hear the excellences of the teacher extolled. The great awards, medals, citations, honorary degrees, and even the higher salaries usually go to the researcher and the author. Not that I think less of the research scholar, but more of the teaching scholar who can touch a spark to the mind of youth and cause it to take fire. Nearly every good mind has to be ignited, and it has usually been some powerful teacher who has been the sparkplug.

We have placed so much emphasis in recent years upon the importance of research and publication that the professor today almost in self-defense may devote his major effort to this phase of his profession. Salary increases come primarily to those who can bring forth scholarly publications—and sometimes publications not so scholarly, but at least pages of print to show for their efforts. Contrast the efforts of the great teacher with the work of the researcher or author. What concrete evidence does the teacher have to show for his labors, if he has not some publication to attest his worth? His results as a teacher (without published articles) are difficult to demonstrate; they are intangible; they are frequently delayed, and it may be years before the effects of his labors are known. But this teacher, like Mary of the Scriptures, has in my judgment chosen the better part.

I believe that few professors today can get far in their profession unless they do some research and publication. To be sure, a reasonable amount of research makes a good teacher better. My complaint is that too many presidents, deans, and heads of departments push these great teachers into research too far, thus causing them to neglect their teaching. At the University of Kentucky I have seen many a professor, known among the students as an excellent instructor, who has been made to feel very miserable because he has had pressure put upon him to do research whether he wanted to do it or not. In such cases I think the dean is under obligation to assign the teacher who does no research a heavier teaching load than the man who carries a reasonable teaching load and does research also. It makes sense to permit one professor to carry eight or nine hours of teaching and do a reasonable amount of research and writing, while another professor who does no research and publishing is required to carry from twelve to fourteen hours of teaching.

No man should enter the profession of teaching unless he finds joy in this work. To do his best, he should have a passion for teaching. He should be motivated by a feeling akin to that expressed by William Lyon Phelps in his *Autobiography, with Letters* when he says:

> I do not know that I could make entirely clear to an outsider the pleasure I have in teaching. I had rather earn my living by teaching than in any other way. In my mind, teaching is not merely a lifework, a profession, an occupation, a struggle: it is a passion. I love to teach as a painter loves to paint, as a musician loves to play, as a singer loves to sing; as a strong man rejoices to run a race. Teaching is an art—an art so great and so difficult to master that a man or a woman can spend a long life at it, without realizing much more than his limitations and mistakes, and his distance from the ideal.

George Herbert Palmer, distinguished Harvard professor, many years ago wrote a little book entitled *The Ideal Teacher*, a book which should be required reading for every person about to enter the teaching profession. Nothing I have ever read so clearly defines the qualities that a teacher should possess. He says in one part of the book:

> On the whole teaching as a trade is poor and disappointing business. . . . Harvard College pays me for doing what I would gladly pay it for allowing me to do. No professional man, then, thinks of giving according to measure. Once engaged, he gives his best, gives his personal interest, himself. His heart is in his work, and for this no equivalent is possible.

Society, however, should not expect those who teach to work without remuneration. In fact, I believe they should be paid as generously as other members of society; and to go a step further, I see no reason why a college or university should pay a scholarly researcher more than a scholarly teacher. I would even go so far as to say that I see no reason why we should not pay an extremely gifted and scholarly teacher as much as we pay a dean or a president. Probably a university should have at least a few great teachers whose salaries are higher than what any administrative officer receives.

The true rewards of teaching cannot be expressed in money, for they are spiritual, not material. They belong among things not seen, but essentially felt. Nevertheless, since we live in a materialistic world, society places value on things material and probably would not appreciate or respect highly the professor who took the vow of poverty.

Too much emphasis today is placed on the quantity and quality of research that a college teacher produces, while his performance in the classroom is often entirely ignored by his departmental head and his dean. My observation of college professors leads me to the conclusion that on every faculty there are a few men that should teach—and teach only—since they are masters in the classroom, while research is to them a disagreeable chore. There are other professors who have little interest in teaching and who regard the meeting of a class as an interruption of their research. These men probably should devote their full time to research work. The number of staff members employed exclusively in research will necessarily be relatively few. On every campus the great majority will teach and also carry on research, because for most professors, teaching and research complement each other. Research findings furnish the raw material for good teaching. A man can be much more enthusiastic about a facet of truth he has discovered than about a truth some other person has discovered.

Teaching is as old as universities; research as we know it today is a relatively new activity of universities. The early colleges of our country, such as Harvard, William and Mary, Columbia, and Yale, were originally concerned primarily with passing on to youth the accumulated knowledge of mankind with special emphasis upon religion. Very little time and effort were given to the discovery of new knowledge (what we think of today as research) until the passage of the Morrill Act in 1862. This act created land-grant colleges and universities, and provided for the teaching of agriculture and "for the liberal and practical education of the industrial classes." Since that time, great emphasis has been placed on scientific discoveries, especially in agricultural and engineering education, and ultimately in all fields of learning.

Each decade for almost a century the amount of money spent for research by educational institutions has increased, until today hundreds of millions of dollars are expended on research covering the whole gamut of human knowledge. How far will the universities go in their quest for new knowledge? Will this relatively new aspect of one of the functions of the university dilute our teaching? My plea is for a balanced program. Definitely there is a place in every college and university for the superior teacher who will do little or no research, but who can in a masterly way transmit the knowledge and culture of the ages to the youth of our time.

There is always room on every university campus for an Albert Einstein, an Alfred North Whitehead, a John Dewey, an Oswald Spengler, a William James, and an H. C. Urey. These creative scholars should be surrounded by such scientific equipment and books as they need. They should plan their own programs, make their own schedules and report periodically on their results. They should be free from all administrative assignments that frequently encumber faculty members. Their business is to penetrate the unknown world, to discover the unknown. There is plenty of room on every campus for such scholars, but their number is few.

Many of the larger universities have discovered the necessity of establishing university presses in order that their professors and other scholars might have an outlet for their scholarly writings. Some of the great contributions to education today are coming off these presses, since they do not have to depend upon a profit for their existence as do our commercial presses. But some university presses are being used as outlets for scholarly work which contributes little to the store of new knowledge. Here I feel that the quality of the product of university presses is being diluted.

In closing this chapter, I would like to say that I have never sought a college presidency. Twice I was tagged for this position. I have always wanted to be a teacher, and I have been a teacher. I hope that as a president I have been a good teacher.

When I retired as President of the University of Kentucky in September, 1956, I received as a gift a book entitled *Great Teachers*, written by Houston Peterson. This book was given to me by my old friend and former colleague, Dr. Alfred L. Crabb, who inscribed it to "Herman Lee Donovan—who fell from the heights of great teaching to the level of great distinction as a university president." This I regard as the finest compliment that I have ever received.

APPENDIX A

Table 1
THE DEVELOPMENT OF THE UNIVERSITY, 1941-1956

Year ending	Degrees awarded	Faculty members	Student enrollment	Library (volumes added)	Income (dollars)
1941	834	478	6,242	22,701	3,370,405.25
1942	760	514	5,145	18,019	3,702,236.45
1943	544	511	4,168	15,103	4,422,122.26
1944	341	502	3,212	16,310	5,118,252.34
1945	332	553	3,156	14,830	4,456,567.83
1946	554	585	6,105	15,952	4,868,575.21
1947	992	672	8,946	24,674	7,019,193.75
1948	1,311	673	9,991	28,973	8,528,871.45
1949	1,809	743	10,110	28,883	9,035,379.08
1950	2,125	805	10,169	31,584	8,859,114.98
1951	1,216	824	8,915	30,810	9,103,779.69
1952	1,382	801	7,900	30,685	9,249,704.22
1953	1,203	815	7,330	30,450	9,212,357.02
1954	1,158	804	7,313	44,433	9,754,914.51
1955	1,192	810	7,861	31,470	10,582,428.85
1956	1,177	865	8,502	32,234	11,482,729.97

Table 2
BUILDINGS CONSTRUCTED ON THE UNIVERSITY CAMPUS
July 1, 1941—September 1, 1956

Building	Date completed	Purpose	Total Cost (dollars)
Wenner-Gren Aeronautical Research Laboratory	1941	Laboratory, classroom	97,000.00
Coal Research Laboratory	1943	Laboratory	18,902.85
Wildcat Bowling Lanes	1943	Physical Education	52,500.00
Wilford Meats Laboratory	1946	Abattoir, laboratory, farm produce sales	25,984.30
Radio Tower	1946	Broadcasting	6,000.00
Combined Shops Building (temporary)	1947	Experiment Station storage	233,241.75
Chemistry Annex (temporary)	1947	Classroom, laboratory	20,000.00
Cooperstown (temporary—largely razed)	1947	Veterans' housing project	398,600.00
Engineering Annex (temporary)	1947	Classroom, laboratory	38,880.00

APPENDIX A

Table 2—*continued*

Building	Date completed	Purpose	Total Cost (dollars)
Quonset Huts (temporary—razed)	1947	Classroom, storage	25,770.00
Scattered Barracks (temporary—razed)	1947	Veterans' housing project	215,550.00
Shawneetown (temporary—razed)	1947	Veterans' housing project	315,880.00
Shop Storage Building (temporary)	1947	Storage	35,400.00
Social Science Building (temporary)	1947	Classroom, office	97,020.00
Euclid Avenue Classroom Building (temporary)	1947	Classroom, laboratory, office	55,500.00
Psychology Annex (temporary)	1947	Classroom, laboratory, office	20,000.00
Little Commons (temporary)	1947	Cafeteria, storage	37,630.00
Bowman Hall	1947	Men's dormitory	439,256.98
Dairy Center	1948	Classroom, laboratory, barn	167,592.17
Dimock Animal Pathology Building Addition and Hospital	1948	Classroom, laboratory, office	409,190.58
Sheep Barns	1948	Laboratory	5,952.32
Cooper Dairy Products Building Addition	1949	Classroom, laboratory	18,991.79
Fine Arts Building	1949	Classroom, laboratory, office, theater	1,646,965.71
McLean Stadium Addition	1949	Athletics	814,943.66
Service Building	1950	Maintenance Division, Library annex, storage	784,490.75
Memorial Coliseum	1950	Auditorium, physical education, athletics	3,863,762.30
456 Rose Street	1950	Sorority house	74,500.00
476 Rose Street	1950	Sorority house	76,000.00
Central Heating Plant, Annex, Steamlines	1950	Heating system	938,217.42
Grehan Journalism Building	1951	Classroom, laboratory, office, printing plant	411,682.22
Six Dormitories	1954	Fraternity and football houses	710,000.00
Donovan Hall	1954	Men's dormitory	1,531,000.00
Keeneland Hall	1954	Women's dormitory	1,222,000.00
Cooperstown	1956	Married students' housing	2,800,000.00
Holmes Hall	*	Women's dormitory	1,055,332.84
Shawneetown	*	Married students' housing	2,067,185.02
TOTAL			20,730,922.66

* Building planned, but not completed until after September 1, 1956.

APPENDIX A

Table 3
MEAN SALARIES OF THE UNIVERSITY FACULTY
1940-1941, 1946-1947, and 1956-1957

Rank	1940-1941 No.	Salary*	1946-1947 No.	Salary†	1956-1957 No.	Salary†
Department Heads and Professors	85	$3,742	104	$4,594	122	$8,218
Associate Professors	39	2,867	56	3,952	97	6,901
Assistant Professors	57	2,518	61	3,306	97	6,068
Instructors	51	1,828	79	2,641	69	5,208
TOTAL	232		300		385	

* The base salary exclusive of pay for summer teaching. Most of these salaries were for the regular school year only.
† All salaries on a twelve-month basis.

Table 4
PRESIDENTS OF THE UNIVERSITY ALUMNI ASSOCIATION
1941-1942 to 1956-1957

E. C. Elliott	1941-1942	J. Stephen Watkins	1949-1950
G. Lee McClain	1942-1943	Edwin R. Denney	1950-1951
H. D. Palmore	1943-1944	Louis Cox	1951-1952
Grover Creech	1944-1945	William H. Townsend	1952-1953
H. C. Robinson	1945-1946	R. R. Dawson	1953-1954
Chauncey L. Forgey	1946-1947	Newton W. Neel	1954-1955
LeRoy Miles	1947-1948	Homer L. Baker	1955-1956
John R. Bullock	1948-1949	Will Ed Covington	1956-1957

APPENDIX B

ARTICLES OF INCORPORATION
OF THE
UNIVERSITY OF KENTUCKY ATHLETIC ASSOCIATION

KNOW ALL MEN BY THESE PRESENTS that the undersigned residents and citizens of the Commonwealth of Kentucky do associate to form a corporation under and in pursuance to the provisions of Chapter 273, Kentucky Revised Statutes, 1944, with all the rights, privileges and immunities of a corporation organized for educational and scientific purposes, without capital stock, and from which no private pecuniary profit is to be derived, and do adopt the following Articles of Incorporation.

ARTICLE I

NAME

The name of the corporation shall be the University of Kentucky Athletic Association, by which name it may contract and be contracted with, hold and convey property, sue and be sued, and carry on business consistent with its purposes and powers.

ARTICLE II

PLACE OF BUSINESS

The principal office and place of business of said corporation shall be in the City of Lexington, Fayette County, Kentucky.

ARTICLE III

NATURE

The said corporation is to be a non-profit organization with no capital stock and from which no private pecuniary profit shall ever be derived by any officer, member, or other person, except such compensation as may be allowed for services actually rendered. The income of the corporation shall be devoted solely to its educational purposes.

APPENDIX B

ARTICLE IV
PURPOSES

The purpose of the corporation shall be to promote athletics and physical culture; to furnish instruction in, and direction of, these activities; to train and prepare instructors, teachers, coaches and directors of athletics for the public schools of the state; to encourage students at the University of Kentucky and the youth of the State of Kentucky to participate in healthful exercise, recreation, athletic games, sports, exhibitions and contests at the University of Kentucky and at such other places as may be desirable and lawful; and to erect, own, lease, equip and maintain athletic fields, swimming pools, stadia, courts, golf courses, gymnasia, and other lands and buildings suitable for the above purposes. It shall be no part of the purpose, power or activity of the corporation to carry on propaganda or to otherwise attempt to influence legislation.

ARTICLE V
POWERS

The corporation shall have power:

(a) To aid and encourage education, particularly in the fields of physical culture and training, and to furnish instructors, equipment, and other aid for this purpose.

(b) To purchase, lease, receive, own, sell, and convey real and personal property of all kinds, particularly lands, buildings and equipment necessary or convenient for participation in athletic training, games and contests.

(c) To employ instructors, coaches, directors, and other persons necessary for carrying out the purposes of the corporation.

(d) To arrange, hold and conduct amateur athletic exhibitions, games, and contests, and to charge and receive admission fees to the same.

(e) To receive and accept donations by gift or devise, absolutely or in trust, and to acquire in other lawful manner moneys and properties for its maintenance.

(f) To borrow money and to give its notes or other obligations therefor and to secure payment thereof by pledging, assigning or mortgaging any property it may own.

(g) To provide for membership of persons interested in the purposes of the association and to issue certificates therefor.

(h) To do any or all other lawful acts reasonably necessary to carry out the objects and purposes of the corporation.

ARTICLE VI

BOARD OF DIRECTORS

The affairs and business of the corporation shall be conducted by a Board of Directors which shall consist of the President of the University of Kentucky and ten other directors appointed by him for a term of one year, five of whom shall be members of the faculty of the University of Kentucky, one shall be the President of the Student Government Association of the University of Kentucky, one shall be an alumnus of the University, and one shall be a member of the Board of Trustees of the University of Kentucky. No person so appointed shall continue in office after he has ceased to be an active member of the Board of Trustees of the University of Kentucky. No person so appointed shall continue in office after he has ceased to be an active member of the group from which he was appointed. The Board of Directors shall adopt by-laws to provide for the internal control and government of the corporation and shall have the power to amend and repeal the same by a vote of the majority of the Board.

ARTICLE VII

OFFICERS

The President of the University, or the person acting as such, by whatever title designated, shall be president of the corporation.

The Board of Directors shall, in the manner provided in the by-laws, elect a Vice President from its membership, and a Secretary and a Treasurer who need not be a member of the Board of Directors. The offices of Secretary and Treasurer may be combined and held by one person. The terms and duties of all officers shall be as provided in the by-laws. The Board of Directors may, from time to time, establish and provide for other officers and employees and prescribe their duties.

ARTICLE VIII

LIMITATION OF INDEBTEDNESS

The highest amount of indebtedness or liability which the corporation may at any time incur shall be $500,000.00.

ARTICLE IX

EXEMPTION FROM LIABILITY

The private property of members of this corporation shall be exempt from liability for any and all debts of the corporation.

APPENDIX B

ARTICLE X

DURATION—DISSOLUTION

The corporation shall exist for a period of fifty years unless sooner dissolved by a vote of two thirds of its Board of Directors, and may be renewed and extended from time to time for further periods of years by a majority vote of the members of its Board of Directors. In the event of the dissolution of the corporation, all of its property, real, personal and mixed and wheresoever situated shall vest immediately and absolutely in the Kentucky Research Foundation subject to all the limitations and uses by which it is held by the corporation at the time of its dissolution. None of the property of the corporation shall ever inure to the benefit of any officer or member of the corporation or other individual.

IN TESTIMONY WHEREOF witness our hands this *20th* day of *November,* 1945.

> [s] *Frank Murray*
> [s] *H. L. Donovan*
> [s] *Maurice F. Seay*
> [s] *Herbert P. Riley*
> [s] *D. V. Terrell*
> [s] *James W. Martin*
> [s] *Thomas D. Clark*

AGREEMENT BETWEEN THE BOARD OF TRUSTEES OF THE UNIVERSITY OF KENTUCKY AND THE UNIVERSITY OF KENTUCKY ATHLETIC ASSOCIATION

BY THIS AGREEMENT entered into in duplicate this 24th day of November, 1945, by and between the Board of Trustees of the University of Kentucky, a corporation, party of the first part, and the University of Kentucky Athletic Association, a corporation, party of the second part, it is mutually understood and agreed:

That in consideration of the sum of One Dollar ($1.00) and other valuable considerations paid to the party of the first part, the receipt of which is hereby acknowledged, and in the further consideration of the covenants of the party of the second part herein contained and of the many advantages and benefits to the University of Kentucky and the students thereof, the party of the first part agrees to allow the party of the second part to use the property known as Stoll Field, including the football and baseball playing and practice fields and McLean Stadium and the Alumni Gymnasium, for the purpose of preparing for and holding athletic exhibitions and contests and to collect admission fees thereto, and to allow the second party to use the athletic equipment now used in the practice for and playing of, such contests.

The party of the second part agrees to employ sufficient and competent instructors and coaches for athletic teams composed of students at the University of Kentucky; to conduct in a careful and proper manner athletic contests with approved teams representing other colleges and schools, and with other teams approved by the first party; to make special concessions to the students of the University of Kentucky in respect to admission to such exhibitions and contests; to keep the above described property in a safe and proper condition so that it may be used by the students of the University of Kentucky for recreational purposes; to save the first party harmless against any and all claims that may arise because of the condition of the property or the manner in which contests and exhibitions are conducted; and, on demand of the party of the first part, to surrender and return the above described property to the party of the first part in as good condition as it was received, reasonable wear and tear and loss or injury due to casualty excepted.

UNIVERSITY OF KENTUCKY
ATHLETIC ASSOCIATION
(Party of the second part)
(Signed) *By H. L. Donovan*

ATTEST: *W. D. Funkhouser*

BOARD OF TRUSTEES OF THE
UNIVERSITY OF KENTUCKY
(Party of the first part)
(Signed) *By Richard C. Stoll*
Chairman of the
Executive Committee

APPENDIX C

READING ASSIGNMENT FOR COLLEGE PRESIDENTS

IN RESPONSE to many requests that I make available the titles of autobiographies and biographies of college and university presidents that I have collected over a period of three decades, I am glad to publish these lists. I am adding the histories of a few institutions of higher education, since most of such histories contain brief biographical sketches of their presidents. I am including the titles of certain other books, mainly autobiographies of teachers, from which I have received great inspiration.

I have been surprised to discover how few biographies of college presidents have been written. I have diligently searched for such books, and I propose to continue the search. Many older biographies, of course, are out of print and are hard to find.

I started the collection in 1928 for a very practical reason—to learn how other college presidents had faced their problems in administering their institutions. I found the study of their lives fascinating, and from their stories I have learned much that has been extremely helpful to me. What started out as a plan to secure useful information on college administration has turned out to be a hobby that has given me great pleasure through the years. I recommend to new college presidents that they obtain eight or ten well-selected autobiographies and biographies, and read them as soon as possible after their appointment. I can guarantee that they will enjoy the assignment and find it immensely rewarding.

AUTOBIOGRAPHICAL

James Burrill Angell, *From Vermont to Michigan: Correspondence of James Burrill Angell, 1869-1871*, edited by Wilfred B. Shaw. Ann Arbor, University of Michigan Press, 1936.

Henry Stites Barker, *Henry Stites Barker: A Selection of Speeches & Other Writings by the Second President of the University of Kentucky*, edited by Ezra L Gillis. Lexington, University of Kentucky Press, 1956.

John Bascom, *Things Learned by Living*. New York, G. P. Putnam's Sons, 1913.

Daniel Bliss, *The Reminiscences of Daniel Bliss*, edited by Frederick J. Bliss. New York, Fleming H. Revell Company, 1920.

William Lowe Bryan, *The Spirit of Indiana: Commencement Addresses, 1902-1917, and Earlier Addresses*. Bloomington, Indiana, University Bookstore, 1917.

Nicholas Murray Butler, *Across the Busy Years: Recollections and Reflections*. 2 vols. New York, Charles Scribner's Sons, 1939-1940.

Lotus D. Coffman, *The State University, Its Work and Problems: A Selection from Addresses Delivered between 1921 and 1923*. London, Oxford University Press, 1934.

Clarence R. and Mary Bell Decker, *A Place of Light: The Story of a University Presidency*. New York, Hermitage House, 1954.

Harold W. Dodds, *Out of This Nettle, Danger*. Princeton, Princeton University Press, 1943.

Timothy Dwight, *Memories of Yale Life and Men, 1854-1899*. New York, Dodd, Mead and Company, 1903.

Charles W. Eliot, *Charles W. Eliot: The Man and His Beliefs*, edited by William Allan Neilson, 2 vols. New York, Harper and Brothers, 1926.

Charles W. Eliot, *Harvard Memories*. Cambridge, Harvard University Press, 1923.

William Goodell Frost, *For the Mountains: An Autobiography*. New York, Fleming H. Revell Company, 1937.

Yukichi Fukuzawa, *The Autobiography of Yukichi Fukuzawa*, translated by Eiichi Kiyooka. Tokyo, Hokuseido Press, 1948.

G. Stanley Hall, *Life and Confessions of a Psychologist*. New York, D. Appleton and Company, 1923.

Alfred Holbrook, *Reminiscences of the Happy Life of a Teacher*. Cincinnati, Elem Street Printing Company, 1885.

Jennie E. Howard, *In Distant Climes and Other Years*. Buenos Aires, American Press, 1931.

Thornwell Jacobs, *Step Down, Dr. Jacobs: The Autobiography of an Autocrat*. Atlanta, Westminster Publishers, 1945.

Burris Jenkins, *Where My Caravan Has Rested*. Chicago, Willett, Clark & Company, 1939.

APPENDIX C   147

E. E. Constance Jones, *As I Remember: An Autobiographical Ramble.* London, A. & C. Black, 1922.

David Starr Jordan, *The Days of a Man: Being Memories of a Naturalist, Teacher and Minor Prophet of Democracy.* 2 vols. Yonkers-on-Hudson, New York, World Book Company, 1922.

Dexter Merriam Keezer, *The Light That Flickers: A View of College Education Which Contrasts Promise and Performance and Suggests Improvements.* New York, Harper & Brothers, 1947.

David Kinley, *The Autobiography of David Kinley.* Urbana, University of Illinois Press, 1949.

Philip Lindsley, *The Works of Philip Lindsley, D.D.* 3 vols. Philadelphia, J. B. Lippincott and Co., 1859.

A. Lawrence Lowell, *What A University President Has Learned.* New York, Macmillan Company, 1938.

James McCosh, *The Life of James McCosh: A Record Chiefly Autobiographical,* edited by William Milligan Sloane. New York, Charles Scribner's Sons, 1897.

Henry Noble MacCracken, *The Hickory Limb.* New York, Charles Scribner's Sons, 1950.

Richard McIlwaine, *Memories of Three Score Years and Ten.* New York, Neale Publishing Company, 1908.

Frank LeRond McVey, *A University Is a Place . . . a Spirit.* Lexington, University of Kentucky Press, 1944.

Robert A. Millikan, *The Autobiography of Robert A. Millikan.* New York, Prentice-Hall, 1950.

Mark Pattison, *Memoirs.* London, Macmillan and Company, 1885.

John Howard Raymond, *Life and Letters of John Howard Raymond,* edited by Harriet Raymond Lloyd. New York, Fords, Howard, and Hulbert, 1881.

Ezekiel Gilman Robinson, *Ezekiel Gilman Robinson: An Autobiography,* edited by E. H. Johnson. New York, Silver, Burdett and Company, 1896.

Peter Sammartino, *The President of a Small College.* Rutherford, New Jersey, Fairleigh Dickinson College Press, 1954.

Henry Nelson Snyder, *An Educational Odyssey.* New York, Abingdon-Cokesbury Press, 1947.

Julian M. Sturtevant, *Julian M. Sturtevant: An Autobiography.* New York, Fleming H. Revell Company, 1896.

Booker T. Washington, *Up from Slavery: An Autobiography*. Garden City, New York, Doubleday, Doran & Company, 1942.

Andrew Dickson White, *Autobiography of Andrew Dickson White*. 2 vols. New York, Century Company, 1905.

BIOGRAPHICAL

Evelyn Abbott and Lewis Campbell, *The Life and Letters of Benjamin Jowett, M.A., Master of Balliol College, Oxford*. 2 vols. London, John Murray, 1897.

Ray Stannard Baker, *Woodrow Wilson: Life and Letters*. Vol II, *Princeton, 1890-1910*. Garden City, New York, Doubleday, Page and Company, 1927.

James Marcus Bledsoe, *A History of Mayo and His College*. Commerce, Texas, 1946.

John William Burgon, *Lives of Twelve Good Men*. New York, Scribner and Welford, 1891.

Varnum Lansing Collins, *President Witherspoon: A Biography*. 2 vols. Princeton, Princeton University Press, 1925.

Kitty Conroy, *George Colvin, Kentucky Statesman and Educator*. Lexington, University of Kentucky, 1944.

Robert C. Cook, editor, *Presidents of American Colleges and Universities*. New York, Robert C. Cook Company, 1933.

George R. Crooks, *The Life of Bishop Matthew Simpson, of the Methodist Episcopal Church*. New York, Harper & Brothers, 1890.

Charles E. Cuningham, *Timothy Dwight, 1752-1817: A Biography*. New York, Macmillan Company, 1942.

Josephus Daniels, *The Life of Woodrow Wilson, 1856-1924*. Philadelphia, John C. Winston Company, 1924.

Elam Franklin Dempsey, *Life of Bishop Dickey*. Nashville, Publishing House of the Methodist Episcopal Church, South, 1937.

J. H. Denison, *Mark Hopkins: A Biography*. New York, Charles Scribner's Sons, 1935.

George Harrison Durand, *Joseph Ward of Dakota*. Boston, Pilgrim Press, 1913.

William Dunseath Eaton and Harry C. Read, *Woodrow Wilson: His Life and Works*. Atlanta, R. L. Phillips Publishing Company, 1919.

APPENDIX C

Charlotte C. Eliot, *William Greenleaf Eliot*, Boston, Houghton Mifflin and Company, 1904.

Abraham Flexner, *Daniel Coit Gilman, Creator of the American Type of University*. New York, Harcourt, Brace and Company, 1946.

Abraham Flexner, *Henry S. Pritchett: A Biography*, New York, Columbia University Press, 1943.

Fabian Franklin, *The Life of Daniel Coit Gilman*. New York, Dodd, Mead and Company, 1910.

Thomas Wakefield Goodspeed, *William Rainey Harper, First President of the University of Chicago*. Chicago, University of Chicago Press, 1928.

Morris Hadley, *Arthur Twining Hadley*. New Haven, Yale University Press, 1948.

Clyde Kenneth Hyder, *Snow of Kansas: The Life of Francis Huntington Snow, with Extracts from His Journals and Letters*. Lawrence, University of Kansas Press, 1953.

Henry James, *Charles W. Eliot, President of Harvard University, 1869-1909*. 2 vols. Boston, Houghton Mifflin Company, 1930.

W. Fletcher Johnson, *The Life of General William Tecumseh Sherman*. Philadelphia, A. T. Hubbard, 1891.

Romie D. Judd, *The Educational Contributions of Horace Holley*. Nashville, George Peabody College for Teachers, 1936.

William M. Landeen, *E. O. Holland and the State College of Washington*. Pullman, State College of Washington, n.d.

Robert E. Lee, Jr., *Recollections and Letters of General Robert E. Lee*. Garden City, New York, Garden City Publishing Company, 1924.

Charles Lee Lewis, *Philander Priestley Claxton, Crusader for Public Education*. Knoxville, University of Tennessee Press, 1948.

Burt Weed Loomis, *The Educational Influence of Richard Edwards*. Nashville, George Peabody College for Teachers, 1932.

Isabel McKinney, *Mr. Lord: The Life and Words of Livingston C. Lord*. Urbana, University of Illinois Press, 1937.

Dumas Malone, *Edwin A. Alderman: A Biography*. New York, Doubleday, Doran & Company, 1940.

Mary Peabody Mann, *Life of Horace Mann*. Washington, D.C., National Education Association, 1937.

APPENDIX C

Massachusetts Department of Education, *Horace Mann Centennial, 1837-1937*. Boston, Walter A. Smith Company, 1937.

George S. Merriam, editor, *Noah Porter: A Memorial by Friends*. New York, Charles Scribner's Sons, 1893.

Edwin Mims, *Chancellor Kirkland of Vanderbilt*. Nashville, Vanderbilt University Press, 1940.

Joy Elmer Morgan, *Horace Mann at Antioch*. Washington, D.C., Horace Mann Centennial Fund, National Education Association, 1938.

James Phinney Munroe, *A Life of Francis Amasa Walker*. New York, Henry Holt and Company, 1923.

James O. Murray, *Francis Wayland*. Boston, Houghton Mifflin and Company, 1891.

George Herbert Palmer, *The Life of Alice Freeman Palmer*. Boston, Houghton Mifflin Company, 1908.

Clyde W. Park, *Ambassador to Industry: The Idea and Life of Herman Schneider*. Indianapolis, Bobbs-Merrill Company, 1943.

Francis Parsons, *Six Men of Yale*. New Haven, Yale University Press, 1939.

James E. Pollard, *William Oxley Thompson, Evangel of Education*. Columbus, Ohio State University, 1955.

Mabel Hardy Pollitt, *A Biography of James Kennedy Patterson*. Louisville, Westerfield-Bonte Company, 1925.

Edmund Quincy, *Life of Josiah Quincy of Massachusetts*. Boston, Ticknor and Fields, 1867.

John Clark Ridpath, *The Life and Work of James A. Garfield*. Cincinnati, Jones Brothers and Company, 1881.

Frederick Rudolph, *Mark Hopkins and the Log: Williams College, 1836-1872*. New Haven, Yale University Press, 1956.

Arthur Marvin Shaw, *William Preston Johnston: A Transitional Figure of the Confederacy*. Baton Rouge, Louisiana State University Press, 1943.

Shirley W. Smith, *James Burrill Angell*. University of Michigan Press, 1954.

William Benjamin Smith, *James Kennedy Patterson*. Manuscript never published.

APPENDIX C 151

Teachers College, Columbia University, *William Fletcher Russell, 1890-1956, Memorial.* New York, Teachers College, 1956.

C. T. Thomson, editor, *Lindsay Hughes Blanton: An Appreciation of His Life and Work.* Lexington, Transylvania Press, 1908.

C. Van Santvoord, *Memoirs of Eliphalet Nott, D.D., LL.D., for Sixty-Two Years President of Union College.* New York, Sheldon & Company, 1876.

Marcus M. Wilkerson, *Thomas Duckett Boyd: The Story of a Southern Educator.* Baton Rouge, Louisiana State University Press, 1935.

John Edwin Windrow, *John Berrien Lindsley, Educator, Physician, Social Philosopher.* Chapel Hill, University of North Carolina Press, 1938.

David Walker Woods, Jr., *John Witherspoon.* New York, Fleming H. Revell Company, 1906.

HISTORICAL

Earl D. Babst and Lewis G. Vander Velder, editors, *Michigan and the Cleveland Era.* Ann Arbor, University of Michigan Press, 1948.

Enoch Albert Bryan, *Historical Sketch of the State College of Washington, 1890-1925.* Spokane, Alumni and the Associated Students, 1928.

Waller Raymond Cooper, *Southwestern at Memphis, 1848-1948.* Richmond, John Knox Press, 1949.

James P. Cornette, *A History of the Western Kentucky State Teachers College.* Bowling Green, Teachers College Heights, 1938.

E. Merton Coulter, *College Life in the Old South.* New York, Macmillan Company, 1928.

Thomas Evans Coulton, *A City College in Action: Struggle and Achievement at Brooklyn College, 1930-1955.* New York, Harper & Brothers, 1955.

Merle Curti and Vernon Carstensen, *The University of Wisconsin: A History, 1848-1925.* 2 vols. Madison, University of Wisconsin Press, 1949.

Jonathan T. Dorris, editor, *Five Decades of Progress: Eastern Kentucky State College, 1906-1957.* Richmond, Eastern Kentucky State College, 1957.

APPENDIX C

J. H. Easterby, *A History of the College of Charleston, Founded 1770.* Charleston, Scribner Press, 1935.

Gilbert E. Govan and James W. Livingood, *The University of Chattanooga: Sixty Years.* Chattanooga, University of Chattanooga, 1947.

James Gray, *The University of Minnesota, 1851-1951.* Minneapolis, University of Minnesota Press, 1951.

Daniel Walker Hollis, *University of South Carolina.* Vol. I, *South Carolina College.* Columbia, University of South Carolina Press, 1951.

Walter Wilson Jennings, *Transylvania, Pioneer University of the West.* New York, Pageant Press, 1955.

Kentucky Writers' Project of the Work Projects Administration, *A Centennial History of the University of Louisville.* Louisville, University of Louisville, 1939.

James O. Knauss, *The First Fifty Years: A History of Western Michigan College of Education, 1903-1953.* Kalamazoo, Western Michigan College of Education, 1953.

Madison Kuhn, *Michigan State: The First Hundred Years, 1855-1955.* East Lansing, Michigan State University Press, 1955.

David A. Lockmiller, *The Consolidation of the University of North Carolina.* Raleigh, University of North Carolina, 1942.

Frank L. McVey, *The Gates Open Slowly: A History of Education in Kentucky.* Lexington, University of Kentucky Press, 1949.

Brander Matthews and others, *A History of Columbia University, 1754-1904.* New York, Columbia University Press, 1904.

Nathaniel Moore, *A Historical Sketch of Columbia College,* revised by J. H. Van Amringe. New York, Columbia College, 1876.

Rosamond Sawyer Moxon and Mabel Clarke Peabody, *Twenty-Five Years.* New Brunswick, New Jersey College for Women, Rutgers University, 1943.

Ohio State University, *Addresses and Proceedings of the Seventy-Fifth Anniversary, 1948-49.* Columbus, Ohio State University Press, 1951.

Charles G. Osgood, *Lights in Nassau Hall: A Book of the Bicentennial, Princeton, 1746-1946.* Princeton, Princeton University Press, 1951.

Elisabeth L. Peck, *Berea's First Century, 1855-1955.* Lexington, University of Kentucky Press, 1955.

George Sessions Perry, *The Story of Texas A and M*. New York, McGraw-Hill Book Company, 1951.

George Wilson Pierson, *Yale: College and University, 1871-1937*. 2 vols. New Haven, Yale University Press, 1952-1955.

David Putnam, *A History of the Michigan State Normal School*. Ypsilanti, Scharf Tag, Label & Box Co., 1899.

James B. Sellers, *History of the University of Alabama, 1818-1902*. University, University of Alabama Press, 1953.

Swarthmore College, *An Adventure in Education: Swarthmore College under Frank Aydelotte*. New York, Macmillan Company, 1941.

Vanderbilt University, *The Inauguration of Oliver C. Carmichael as Chancellor of Vanderbilt University*. Nashville, Vanderbilt University, 1938.

Vanderbilt University, *Proceedings of the Semi-Centennial of Vanderbilt University*. Nashville, Vanderbilt University, 1926.

Henry McGilbert Wagstaff, *Impressions of Men and Movements at the University of North Carolina*. Chapel Hill, University of North Carolina Press, 1950.

Louis R. Wilson, The University of North Carolina, 1900-1930: The Making of a Modern University. Chapel Hill, University of North Carolina Press, 1957.

James Albert Woodburn and Burton Dorr Myers, *History of Indiana University*. 2 vols. Bloomington, Indiana University, 1940-1952.

INSPIRATIONAL

Victor Lincoln Albjerg, *Richard Owen, Scotland, 1810–Indiana, 1890*. Lafayette, Archives of Purdue, 1946.

Robert M. Bartlett, *They Dared To Live*. New York, Association Press, 1937.

Charles Albert Blanchard, *Going to College*. Wheaton, Illinois, Wheaton College, n.d.

Mary Ellen Chase, *A Goodly Fellowship*. New York, Macmillan Company, 1939.

Wilbur L. Cross, *Connecticut Yankee: An Autobiography*. New Haven, Yale University Press, 1943.

Edward Howard Griggs, *The Story of an Itinerant Teacher*. Indianapolis, Bobbs-Merrill Company, 1934.

APPENDIX C

James Hilton, *Good-bye, Mr. Chips*. Boston, Little, Brown, and Company, 1934.

Louis Edward Holden, *Why Go to College?* Wooster, Ohio, University of Wooster, n.d.

Henry Johnson, *The Other Side of Main Street: A History Teacher from Sauk Centre*. New York, Columbia University Press, 1943.

Lee Kirkpatrick, *Teaching School Day by Day*. Lexington, Kentucky, Hobson Press, 1941.

Walter Hines Page, *The School That Built a Town*. New York, Harper & Brothers, 1952.

Alice Freeman Palmer, *Why Go to College?* New York, Thomas Y. Crowell & Company, 1897.

George Herbert Palmer, *The Ideal Teacher*. Boston, Houghton Mifflin Company, 1910.

Frances Gray Patton, *Good Morning, Miss Dove*. New York, Dodd, Mead & Company, 1954.

William Alexander Percy, *Lanterns on the Levee: Recollections of a Planter's Son*. New York, Alfred A. Knopf, 1941.

Bliss Perry, *And Gladly Teach: Reminiscences*. Boston, Houghton Mifflin Company, 1935.

Bliss Perry, editor, *The Heart of Emerson's Journals*. Boston, Houghton Mifflin Company, 1926.

William Lyon Phelps, *Autobiography, with Letters*. New York, Oxford University Press, 1939.

A. H. Redford, *Life and Times of H. H. Kavanaugh, D.D.* Nashville, 1884.

Anna Perrott Rose, *The Gentle House*. Boston, Houghton Mifflin Company, 1954.

George Santayana, *Persons and Places*. 2 vols. New York, Charles Scribner's Sons, 1944-1945.

Albert Schweitzer, *Out of My Life and Thought: An Autobiography*. New York, Henry Holt and Company, 1949.

Nathaniel Southgate Shaler, *The Autobiography of Nathaniel Southgate Shaler*. Boston, Houghton Mifflin Company, 1909.

Vincent Sheean, *Lead, Kindly Light*. New York, Random House, 1949.

Horace Dutton Taft, *Memories and Opinions*. New York, Macmillan Company, 1942.

G. Ernest Thomas, *To Whom Much Is Given: The Stewardship Questions of Jesus*. New York, Abingdon-Cokesbury Press, 1946.

Guy Montrose Whipple, *How to Study Effectively*. Bloomington, Illinois, Public-School Publishing Company, 1916.

INDEX

Adult and Extension Education, College of: 50. *See also* Extension Education, Department of
Agricultural and Industrial Development Board: 65
Agricultural and Mechanical College: 38, 67
Agricultural Engineers: 48
Agricultural Experiment Station: 43, 64, 125
Agricultural Extension Service: 43, 63, 64, 125
Agriculture and Home Economics, College of: 43, 44, 48, 58, 64-65, 125
Agronomy, Department of: 38-39
Alumni Gymnasium: 34
Alumni Relations: interest in Alumni clubs, 61-63; interest in athletics: 34, 62, 106, 115; raising money for campus building, 34; interpreting University to public, 66; Alumni Association, 61, 62, 63; presidents of Alumni Association, 1941-1956, 63, 139; on UKAA board of directors, 106
Amendment of Kentucky Constitution, Art. 246, failed to pass, 24; passed, 26
American Association of Colleges of Teacher Education: 71-72
American Association of University Professors: 72
American Medical Association: 52, 55
Anderson Collection: Library, 119
Ardery, Judge William B.: 21, 24, 74-75
Army Specialized Training Program: 58
Arts and Sciences, College of: 38, 46, 48
Assembly (University): 7

Association of Governing Boards of State Universities: 81
Association of Research Libraries: 118
Athletic Association, University of Kentucky: reasons for formation, 105; peculiar functions, 105-107; Articles of Incorporation, 105-106, 140-43; Articles of Agreement, 105-106, 143-44; Board of Directors, UKAA, 106
Athletics in the University: in early days, 102, 103; improvement in ethical standards, 103; athletic scholarships and grants-in-aid, 110; sports programs in public relations, 62, 108, 109, 111-12; importance of Conferences, 115, 116; difficulty in administration of athletic program, 110-11; basketball scandal, 112-16; Director of Athletics, 6, 8; Memorial Coliseum, 19, 34-35, 59. *See also:* Basketball, Football
Attorney General (Kentucky): 95, 105
Atwood, President Rufus B.: 100
Automobile: as enemy of scholarship, 90-91, 94

Baker, Merl: 124
Bankers, School for: 65
Baptists, General Association of: requests Bible courses in University, 76
Barker, President Henry Stites: 38, 51
Barkley, Senator Alben W.: papers and mementos, 119-20; Barkley Room in Library, 120
Basketball in University: 62, 106, 107, 109, 112-16
Bible teaching requested: 76-77
Biennial brochure on budget: 17
Blanding, Miss Sarah: dean of women, 88

INDEX

Board of Trustees: on governing regulations, 4, 7; relations with President, 1, 2, 3, 4, 12-14, 46; on finances, 7, 16-17, 46, 83; on Haggin Trust Fund, 19, 41; on bond issues for buildings, 30, 35; on State control of salaries and appointments, 71-72; on open minutes, 85; on integration, 96-98; on School of Pharmacy, 47; on increased extension service, 49-50; on athletics, 108, 115; on UKAA, 106; on appointments, 44, 55; on Medical Center, 54; on charges in Aeronautical Laboratory case, 74-75
Bond issues for construction: 30, 33, 35, 107
Bowman Hall: 33
Bradley Hall: 91
Brewer, Colonel B. E.: Commandant, ROTC: 57
Bryant, Paul: football coach, 108
Budget (University): preparing, 5, 7, 16-17; defense of, 17; biennial budget brochure, 17; decreasing power of trustees in budget making, 83; introducing budget to public, 17, 61
Building on campus, 1941-56: 28, 30-31, 33-35, 47-48, 54, 137-38
Bureau of Source Materials in Higher Education: Library, 120
Burley Tobacco Growers Cooperative Association: 125

Campus (University): 63, 89, 93, 114
Campus Book Store: 47
Canadiana: Library, 119
Capitol: law library in, 96
Carpenter, C. C.: dean, 65, 87
Chamber of Commerce: 65
Chamberlain, Leo M.: Vice President of University, 4, 9-11, 75, 121, 124
Chandler, Governor A. B.: trustee, 16, 17, 54, 55
Chemical Engineers: 48
Clark, Thomas D.: 120
Classrooms: 29, 30, 33, 137-38
Clay, Henry: Papers (Library), 119
Clements, Governor Earle C.: trustee, 35, 97-98

Code of governing regulations: 3-5, 7
Collier, Blanton: coach, 108
Commerce, College of: 65
Commission, Legislative Research: study of need for new medical school, 53
Commissioner of Finance (State): 16, 21
Committee of Fifteen: work on code of regulations, 3-4, 7
Comptroller: 10, 15, 74
Conferences, athletic: 103, 110, 115, 116
Convocation: 5, 7
Cooper, Thomas Poe: dean, 3, 38, 43-44, 58, 64, 73, 125, Thomas Poe Cooper Agricultural Foundation, 125
Cooperstown: veterans' community, 31-32, 33, 88
Council of State Governments: 80, 82
Court of Appeals (Kentucky): 21, 22, 23, 24, 25-26
Covington: University extension center at, 49-50
Crabb, Alfred L.: 136
Cultural programs in Memorial Coliseum: 34-36
Curriculum: increased offerings in, 40, 77-78; control of, 7, 40, 78; request for Bible courses, 76-77

Dawson, Judge Charles I.: 25-26
Day Law: 95, 96, 97, 98
Dean of Men: 8, 86, 89, 90, 99
Dean of University: 8, 9, 86
Dean of Women: 8, 86, 89, 90, 99
Degrees given: 16, 137
Delegation of authority: 6, 8, 83
Denbo, Bruce F.: director, University Press, 122
Department of Finance (Kentucky): 71, 83
Development of University: 16, 28-29, 63, 83, 100, 117-19, 121, 123-25, 135, 137
Dickey, President Frank G.: 55, 65
Director of Athletics: 107, 108
Discipline on University campus: 5, 7, 88, 90-91, 93-94, 103, 110, 114-16
Distinguished professorships: 43

INDEX 159

Donnell, Colonel Howard: 57
Donovan, President Herman L.:
—biographical, early life, 63, 127-29; in college, 129-30; as farmer, 63-64
—view of duties as President, 1, 2, 6-8, 12
—relations with faculty, 1-2, 4, 18, 37, 39, 40, 41, 43, 44, 55, 139
—relations with alumni, 34, 61-68
—relations with students, 85, 90
—relations with veterans, 31-33
—public relations, 17, 22-23, 60-61, 66-67
—relations with board of trustees, 1, 2, 3, 4, 12-14
—on financing, 15-17
—on athletics, 104, 106, 108-116
—on teaching and research: 43, 62, 127-36
—resisting pressures, 44, 64-65, 69, 70-75, 77-78, 85, 90, 125
—on Library, 118, 119
—on relations with private colleges, 68
—on Memorial Coliseum, 34
—on Keeneland Foundation, 23-24
—on Medical Center, 54, 55
Donovan Hall: 33
Drake, Daniel: 50
Dudley, Benjamin: 50

Eastern Kentucky State Teachers' College: 2
Education, College of: 65-66
Engineering, College of: 31, 38, 48, 58, 73
Engineers' Specialist School: 58
Enrollment: 137
"Executive Budget" of State: 80
Extension Education, Department of: 48-50. See also Adult and Extension Education, College of

"Fabulous Five": 112
Faculty: University, 1, 6, 7, 72, 137; subjects of discontent, 1, 2, 18; encouragement of scholarship, 42, 123-25; securing new faculty, 41, 45, 55; value in public relations, 44; pressure upon, 43-44, 69, 70-72;

Faculty (continued):
preparing for integration, 99-100; relations with University Press, 122; teaching and research of faculty, 41-42, 123-24. See also salaries
Farquhar, Edward E.: 130
FBI: 73
Federal Court: 96, 97
Federal Government: 31, 33
Federal Narcotics Bureau: 92
Federal Public Housing Authority: 31, 32, 33
Feuding in University: 1, 38-39, 67-68, 75-76
Financing the University: 15, 16-17, 18-20, 23-24, 41, 46, 122, 123-25
Fine Arts Building: 30
Football in the University: 62, 87, 102, 103, 104-105, 107-108, 109, 112
Ford, Judge H. Church: 96, 97, 98
4-H Clubs: 64
Frazee Hall: 91
Freedom of teaching: 70-72

"Gangsters, junior": 91-94
Garrigus, Wesley: 64
General Assembly (Kentucky): appropriations to University, 16, 17, 19, 34, 35, 47, 71-72, 83, 104-105; endangers University freedom, 20-22; on Day Law, 95; on football, 104; on new Medical Center, 51, 52, 53-54; House report on Aer. Lab. case, 75; on athletics building, 35
Geography, Department of: 46
Gillis, Ezra L: 15-16, 38, 59, 120, 128
Ginger, Lyman V.: dean, 50
Graduate School: 96, 98
Graham, Colonel James H.: dean, 31, 59, 73, 74-75
Grehan, Enoch, Journalism Building: 34, 47
Griffith Collection: Library, 114

Haggin Trust Fund: 19-20, 41, 122
Hammer Collection: Library, 119
Hatch, John W.: 95
Headley, Hal Price: 23-24
Hill, Henry H.: dean, 9

INDEX

Hobson, R. P.: trustee, 98
Hogan, Miss Lucy: 11-12
Holifield, M. B.: Assistant Attorney General, 76-77, 96, 97
Holley, President Horace: 50
Holmes, Mrs. Sarah B.: dean of women, 86, 88, 89
Holmes Hall: 33
Home Economics, School of: 48
Housing for students: temporary, 28-29, 31, 33; permanent, 28-29, 33; for veterans, 29-34; for Negroes, 100; survey of, 137-38
Huguelet, Guy A.: trustee, 104

"The Immortals": 103
Integration: steps into, 98-101
Intelligence agents, War Dept.: 73

James, Senator Ollie: 128, 129
Jewell, Miss Frances (Mrs. F. L. McVey): dean of women, 88
Jewell Hall: 89
Johnson, Governor Keen: trustee, 17, 18-19, 24, 35
Johnson, Lyman T.: 96
Jones, T. T.: dean of men, 86-87
Journalism, School of: 34, 47-48; Enoch Grehan Journalism Building, 34, 47

Keeneland Foundation: 23-24, 30
Keeneland Hall: 33
Kentucky Farm Bureau: 54, 63-64
Kentucky Independent College Foundation (KICF): 68
Kentucky Medical Association: 52, 54
Kentucky Medical Foundation: 54
Kentucky Research Foundation: 122-25
Kentucky State College (Frankfort): 96, 98, 100
Kentucky Utilities: 125
Kernel Press: 47
King, Miss Helen: alumni secretary, 63
King, Miss Margaret I.: librarian, 118, 120
Kinkead Hall: 91
Kirwan, A. D.: dean of men, 86, 87-88, 89, 90, 115-16

Law, College of: 65, 95
Lawsuits of University: testing the $5,000 salary limit, 20-21, 25-27; charges against Col. Graham et al., 74-76; on admission of Negroes, 96-98
Librarian: 6, 8, 121
Library (Building): Carnegie Library, 117; Margaret I. King Library, 118; library annex in Service Building, 34, 118; need for more library space, 119-20
Library (Institution): increasing number of volumes, 117, 118, 119; budget, 119; departmental libraries, 120-21; staff, 119; photographic service, 121; manuscript and rare book collections, 119-20; Library Associates, 121; member, Association of Research Libraries, 118; Department of Archives, 121; Library Committee, 121; survey, 137

McVey, President Frank L.: 2, 19, 29, 38, 48, 51, 56, 67, 73, 117, 118, 119, 122; McVey Papers, Library, 119
Madison Square Garden: 113
Martin, Leslie: dean of men, 86, 90-93
Maxwell Place: 2, 67
Medical Center, Lexington: 10, 16, 47, 51-54; Vice President of, 55
Medical School, Louisville: 52
Memorial Coliseum: financing of, 19, 34, 35, 107; dual purpose, 34-36, 59; cultural programs, 35-36; memorial roster in, 59
Morrill Act: 135
Murray State Teachers' College: 21

NAACP: 96
National Collegiate Athletics Association (NCAA): 103, 110, 115, 116
Negroes: experience in integration, 99-100
Noe, Cotton: 130

O'Rear, Judge Edward C.: trustee, 97-98
"Panty Raids": 89-90

INDEX

Patterson, President James K.: 5-6, 7-8, 51, 85; Patterson collection, Library, 119; Patterson Hall, 33
Pence, M. L.: 130
Personnel director: 6, 8
Peterson, Frank D.: Vice President of Business Affairs, 10, 74, 124
Pharmacy, College of: 46-47, 66
Phoenix Hotel: 58
Physics, Department of: in World War II, 56, 57
Pickett papers: Library, 119
Placement Services: director of, 6, 8
Plock, Richard: 81
Pratt-Whitney Aircraft Corporation: 73
Presidency: 6, 8, 11, 37, 86
The Press: 17, 22-23, 44, 52, 53, 60-61, 72, 107, 108, 112, 114, 115
Press, University of Kentucky: 122; director of, 6, 8, 122
Pressures: 44, 53, 69, 70-75, 77-78
Private colleges: improving relations with, 67-68
Provost: 6
"The Public": 67
Public relations of University: importance of, 60; alumni importance in public relations, 62-63; aid of athletics, 109; with farmers, 64-65, 67; with business men, 65; with lawyers, 65; special value of College of Pharmacy, 66; director of public relations, 6, 8

Radio, relations with: 60, 61, 108, 114
Reading list for college presidents: 2-3, 145-55
Rees, Judge William H.: 22
Regional Athletic Conferences: 103, 110, 116
Registrar: 6
Regulations governing University: 3-4
"Relationship between the State Government and the University of Kentucky: Report and Recommendations, March, 1951": 72
Research: 62, 66, 118, 123, 131-36
Researchers: 134-35
Richardson, William: 50

ROTC: 57
Rupp, Adolph: basketball coach, 107, 112, 114

Salaries: reduction during depression, 17-18; loss of faculty from low salaries, 18, 22, 27, 40-41; 12-month basis, 19; case of $5,000 limit, 20-26; increasing salaries, 41, 45, 139; political menace to salaries, 71, 84; salary aid through certain Foundations, 123-24
Scholarship aid: 42, 90, 123-25
Secretary to President: 10-11
Senate (University): 1-2, 3
Service Building: 34, 118, 121, 137-38
Shawneetown: 31, 34, 88
Slone, Earl P.: dean, 46, 66
Southeastern Conference: 103, 104, 110, 115
Southern Association of Colleges and Secondary Schools: 71-72
Stadium: 30, 107, 114
Stahr, Elvis: dean, 65
Stanley, Judge O. W.: 26
Stoll, Judge Richard C.: trustee, 4, 73, 74, 98, 106
Stores, University: 10
Streit, Judge Saul S.: 114-15
Student Government Association: 70, 89, 90
Student Loan Fund: 86-87
Student Union Building: 100
Students: petition, 75; advice to, 77; financial aid to, 123-24; student pressures on administration, 85-86; importance of keeping them informed, 85; counselors of, 86, 88-90; opinions of, 131; increase in numbers of, 137

Taylor, William S.: dean, 65
Teachers: student evaluation of, 131; pressure for research, 132-33; great teachers, 130
Tenure, presidential: 126-27
Thompson, Lawrence S.: director of Libraries, 120-21
Transylvania Medical School: 50-51
Trout, Allan M.: 44, 72
Trustees. *See* Board of Trustees

Veterans on campus: 30-33, 49-50, 87-88
Vice President: of the University, 6, 8, 16, 89; of Business Administration, 6, 8, 10, 16; of the Medical Center, 8, 10-11, 55
Visual aids: 49

Wall, Bennett: 119
War Department: 56, 57, 59, 73, 74
Webb, W. S.: 56-57, 130
Welch, Frank J.: dean, 64
Wenner-Gren Aeronautical Laboratory: 73-75
Wetherby, Governor Lawrence W.: 114
Willard, William R.: Vice President of the Medical Center, 10-11, 55
Willis, Governor Simeon S.: trustee, 35, 75
Wilson, Samuel: Library, 119, 120
World War II and the University: 36, 56-59, 73, 87, 104. *See also* Veterans on campus

www.ingramcontent.com/pod-product-compliance
Lightning Source LLC
Chambersburg PA
CBHW032047150426
43194CB00006B/446